P9-ELW-410

The Gadabout

Believe it or not, the Gadabout's "whirling pinwheels" are simply squares sewn and cut on the diagonal. The contrasting "hourglass" is made by sewing two 2½" strips together and cutting with the Triangle Square Up Ruler. Lavenders, purples and greens give Marie's Gadabout quilt a contemporary look. Below, a little girl's bed is decorated with the twin quilt by Marie Harper.

Pieced by Marie Harper
Quilted by Carol Selepec
64" x 94"

Still Stripping
After 25 Years

Eleanor Burns

On the Cover

Eleanor celebrates her Silver Anniversary with a trademark "strip toss" against a colorful background of quilts. From the left, clockwise, the Gadabout Quilt, Stars and Four-Patches, and the Cornerstones Quilt show the remarkable versatility of her favorite 2½ inch strips, combined with easy star points and pinwheels made with Quilt in Day's Triangle Square Up and Triangle in a Square rulers. Look inside for a selection of sixteen different strip quilts, ranging from traditional to contemporary designs and featuring 100% cotton fabric from her new Yours Truly line by Benartex, Inc.

For Merritt

The man behind the scenes. Merritt came to Quilt in a Day in 1986, and since then, he's been responsible for taking us from hand-drawn illustrations to the latest in computer graphics. I know I can always count on his dedication and excellence, whether he's designing the cover for my latest book or sitting in for a test photo!

Third printing January, 2004
Published by Quilt in a Day®, Inc.
1955 Diamond St., San Marcos, CA 92069
©2003 by Eleanor A. Burns Family Trust

ISBN 1-891776-14-2

Art Director Merritt Voigtlander
Production Artist Marie Harper

Printed in China. All rights reserved. No part of this material may be reproduced in any form or by any electronic or mechanical means, including information storage and retrieval systems, without permission in writing from the author. The publisher presents the information in this book in good faith. No warranty is given, nor are results guaranteed.

Contents

Introduction

It's amazing what you can do with 2½ inch strips and a sewing machine! It all started in 1978 with my first book, *Make a Quilt in a Day Log Cabin*. Little did I know that this single book was going to launch a fabric store, a television program, and hundreds of thousands of new quilters! Here at my sewing machine, with the company of my "grandpuppies" Peanut and Tabitha, I've spent many happy hours dreaming up new projects. For my twenty-fifth anniversary, I put together a collection of sixteen different quilts made with 2½ inch strips, just like that original Log Cabin.

The quilts in this book are dedicated to the people who helped make my dreams a reality: my sons, Grant and Orion, my sisters, Patricia and Judy, my best friend Brian, and of course, the dedicated staff and teachers who helped make Quilt in a Day a success. After twenty-five years, there are so many stories to tell and memories to share. I hope you enjoy the story these quilts have to tell.

Keep on stripping!

Eleanor Burns

Supplies

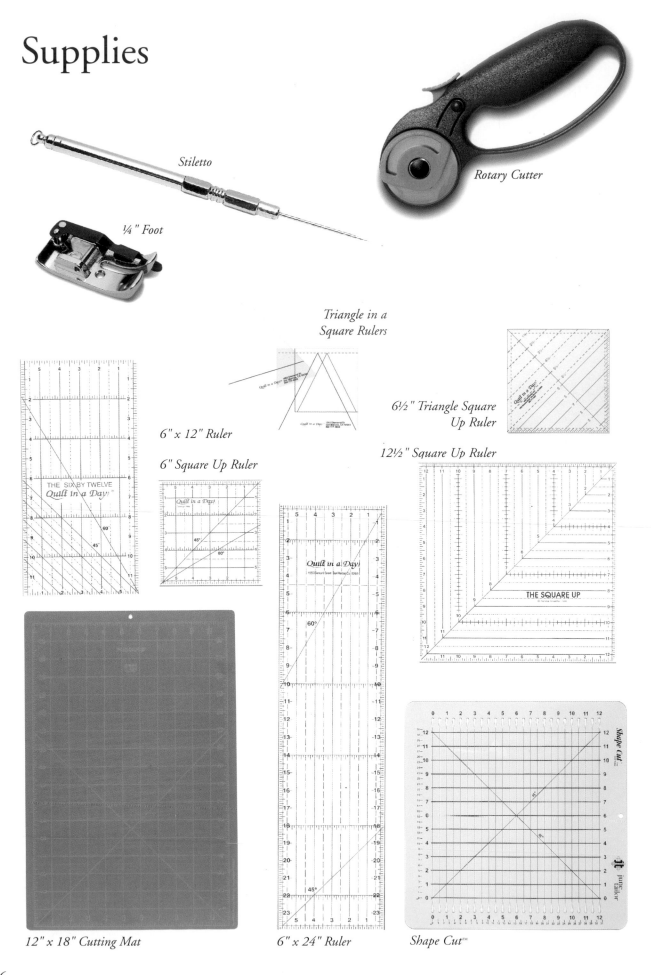

Stiletto

Rotary Cutter

¼ " Foot

Triangle in a
Square Rulers

6" x 12" Ruler

6½ " Triangle Square
Up Ruler

6" Square Up Ruler

12½ " Square Up Ruler

12" x 18" Cutting Mat

6" x 24" Ruler

Shape Cut™

Cutting and Sewing Techniques

Cutting Strips with Ruler and Cutter

1. Cut a nick in one selvage, a tightly woven edge. Tear across the grain from selvage to selvage.

2. Press the fabric, particularly the torn edge.

3. Fold the fabric in half, matching the frayed edges. Don't worry about the selvages not lining up as this is not always possible. Line up the straight of the grain.

4. Place the fabric on the gridded mat with the folded edge along a horizontal line, and the torn edge on a vertical line.

5. Place the quarter inch line of the ruler along the torn edge of the fabric.

6. Spread your fingers and place four on top of the ruler with the little finger on the edge to keep the ruler firmly in place.

7. Take the rotary cutter in your free hand and open the blade. Starting below the fabric, begin cutting away from you, applying pressure on the ruler and the cutter. Keep the blade next to the ruler's edge.

8. Cut strips designated widths. To help you, place Glow-Line™ Tape from Omnigrid along the designated line on your ruler. Open the first strip and look at the fold to see if it is straight. If it has a crook that looks like an elbow, the fabric may not be folded on the straight of the grain. If this happens, repeat the preceding steps.

9. Strips and Borders are cut different widths. Check your particular Yardage Chart for measurements. Suggested widths for Borders are given, but can be changed as long as you get the size quilt you desire. Some fabrics may not look attractive in the widths suggested. Fold the fabric to the finished size and lay them together with the quilt top before cutting all the strips.

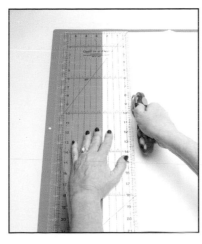

If you are right-handed, the fabric should trail off to the right.

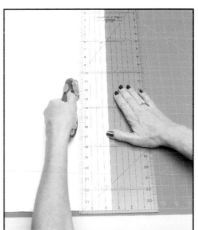

If you are left-handed, the fabric should trail off to the left.

Cutting Strips with Shape Cut™

1. Place Glow-Line™ Tape at designated measurement as 2½", 5", 7½", etc.

2. Fold fabric into fourths, lining up selvage edges with fold.

3. Place Shape Cut™ on fabric. Line up zero horizontal line with bottom edge of fabric. Allow extra fabric to left of zero for straightening.

Line up zero horizontal line with bottom edge of fabric.

4. Place blade of cutter in zero line, and straighten left edge of fabric. Cut strips designated widths.

5. Cut Borders according to Yardage Charts.

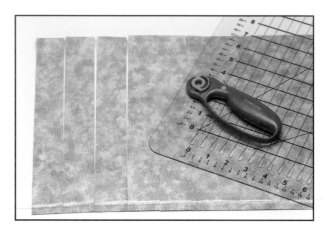

Cut fabric into strips.

Cutting Squares

1. Fold desired fabric into fourths.

2. Cut strips designated widths.

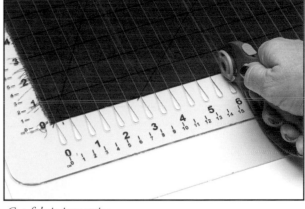

Cut fabric into strips.

3. Turn strip, square off left edge, and cut into desired size squares.

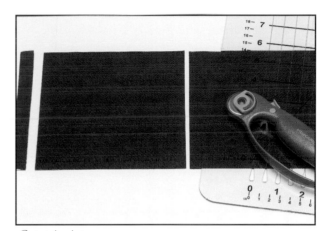

Cut strips into squares.

¼" Seam Allowance Test

Use a consistent ¼" seam allowance throughout the construction of the quilt. If necessary, adjust the needle position, change the presser foot, or feed the fabric under the presser foot to achieve the ¼". Complete the ¼" seam allowance test before starting.

1. Cut three 1½" x 6" pieces.

2. Set machine at 15 stitches per inch, or 2.0 on computerized machines.

3. Sew three strips together lengthwise with what you think is a ¼" seam.

4. Press seams in one direction. Make sure no folds occur at seams.

5. Place sewn sample under a ruler and measure its width. It should measure exactly 3½". If sample measures smaller than 3½", seam is too large. If sample measures larger than 3½", seam is too small. Adjust seam and repeat if necessary.

¼" Foot

Available for most sewing machines, a ¼" foot has a guide on it to help you keep your fabric from straying, giving you perfect ¼" seams. Your patchwork is then consistently accurate.

Pressing

Individual instructions usually say dark fabric should be on top, unless otherwise indicated.

1. Place on pressing mat, with fabric on top that seam is to be pressed toward. Set seam by pressing stitches.

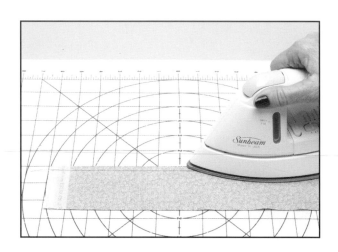

2. Open and press against seam.

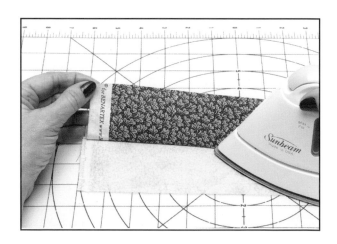

Needles and Stitch Length

Use a fine, sharp, #70/10 needle. Use small stitches, approximately 15 per inch, or 2.0 on computer machines with stitch selections from 1 to 4. Use a machine quilting needle and 10 stitches per inch, or 3.5 on a computer machine when machine quilting.

Neutral Thread

Sew the quilt blocks together with a good quality of neutral shade polyester or cotton spun thread. When machine quilting, use the same color thread as the backing in the bobbin and thread the same color as the fabric on top, or invisible thread. Use quilting thread for hand quilting.

Measuring and Choosing a Pattern

Decide if you want your quilt to only cover the top mattress, or cover to the floor. Decide if you will tuck the pillows in or use pillow shams on top of the quilt. Measure the length and width of what you want covered on your bed.

On most bed quilts in *Still Stripping*, the blocks cover the top mattress, the first border frames the mattress, and the remaining borders hang over the sides. Check the approximate finished sizes at the top of each yardage chart to find the one that is suited to your purpose. You can always design your own fit by increasing or decreasing the number of blocks and borders.

Measure to edge of top mattress for coverlet size. Measure to floor for bedspread size.

Quarter Log Cabin Quilt

Sit down and have a cup of coffee with me. That's exactly what Bill, my husband, and I were doing in 1978 when we conceived the idea of a book to go along with my students' favorite class, making the log cabin quilt. Grant had just gotten a new camera for Christmas, and three-year-old Orion tried it out. Grant, a big boy of five, did a little better framing us up!

Bill was in law school, so it seemed like a good plan to supplement the budget. We worked hard all year, pairing my writing with his illustrations. By December, we had *Make a Quilt in a Day Log Cabin* ready for photocopying and comb binding. Our small ad placed in Family Circle magazine, beside an ad about basement toilets that flush up, brought in enough cash to cover the ad and then some. We were in business! A quarter of a century later, the log cabin quilt is still popular with my students.

Patty's home spun star in tones of cranberry, cream, and navy offer a warm country welcome, perfect for her dining room wall.

Pieced and Quilted by Patricia Knoechel
60" x 60"

With tones of brown sugar and cinnamon, Gloria arranged her blocks in a stunning design to grace her wall. She completed her quilt with a folded border of red, followed by rich brown to perfectly compliment her floral print red border.

Pieced by Gloria Yanik
Quilted by
Nancy Letchworth
60" x 60"

With just sixteen quarter log cabin blocks, you can make a variety of patterns for the Large Wallhanging. Simply make eight blocks from each color family, and build your own design or use one of these layouts.

You can almost feel the wind blowing in Nancy's Windmill Spinner design in shades of blues, reds and laundry fresh whites. Her colors are mirrored in three borders for a picture perfect wallhanging. Nancy used yellow corner square fabric for both families to create the large yellow squares.

Pieced and Quilted by
Nancy Letchworth
60" x 60"

Fabric Selection

Teresa's queen size quilt offers a beautiful display of the Yours Truly fabric line in shades of red, caramel, and green. She framed her artwork in Caramel Rose Remembrance for a perfect finish.

84" x 84"

Pieced by Teresa Varnes
Quilted by Carol Selepec

How to Select Your Fabric

Choose two different color families, as red and green. For each color family, select one fabric that reads solid for Corner, and five additional fabrics in values from medium to dark. Prints should also vary in scale as tone on tone, small, medium, and large scale. If possible, select a few prints that have colors from both families.

Select five Backgrounds in similar values, but varying in scale. Limited touches of color from both families help tie all fabrics together. The five Background fabrics are used for both sets of blocks.

An optional folded border can be used to frame the blocks. For large quilts, select a medium from one color family and a dark from the second family for borders.

Yours Truly
Fabrics by
BENARTEX
INCORPORATED

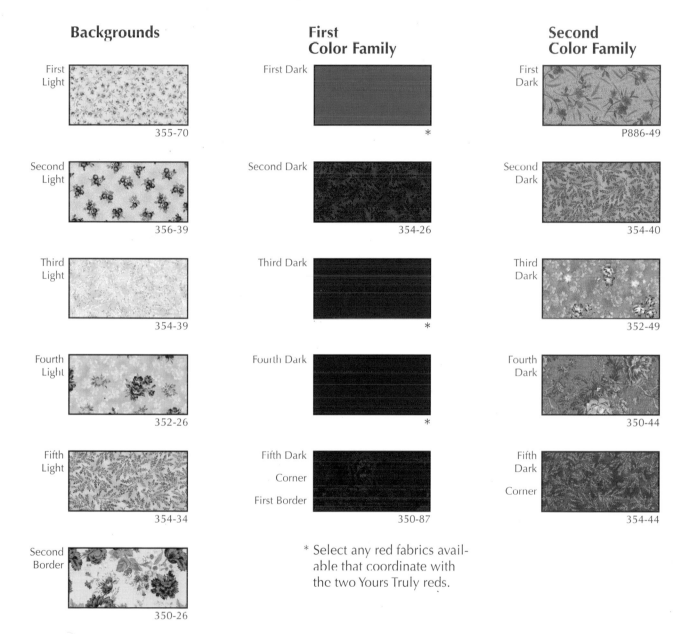

Backgrounds	First Color Family	Second Color Family
First Light	First Dark	First Dark
355-70	*	P886-49
Second Light	Second Dark	Second Dark
356-39	354-26	354-40
Third Light	Third Dark	Third Dark
354-39	*	352-49
Fourth Light	Fourth Dark	Fourth Dark
352-26	*	350-44
Fifth Light	Fifth Dark / Corner / First Border	Fifth Dark / Corner
354-34	350-87	354-44
Second Border		
350-26		

* Select any red fabrics available that coordinate with the two Yours Truly reds.

Yardage

Purchase five different values each for two color families. Light yardage is enough for both color families.

Finished Block Size 12" square	Small Wallhanging 2 x 2 = 4 total 36" x 36"	Large Wallhanging 4 x 4 = 16 total 60" x 60"
First Light*	⅛ yd (1) 2½" strip	¼ yd (2) 2½" strips
Second Light	⅛ yd (1) 2½" strip	¼ yd (2) 2½" strips
Third Light	⅛ yd (1) 2½" strip	⅓ yd (3) 2½" strips
Fourth Light	⅛ yd (1) 2½" strip	⅜ yd (4) 2½" strips
Fifth Light	¼ yd (2) 2½" strips	½ yd (6) 2½" strips
Two Color Families* Corner	⅛ yd of each (1) 2½" strip of each	⅛ yd of each (1) 2½" strip of each
First Dark	⅛ yd of each (1) 2½" strip of each	⅛ yd of each (1) 2½" strip of each
Second Dark	⅛ yd of each (1) 2½" strip of each	¼ yd of each (2) 2½" strips of each
Third Dark	⅛ yd of each (1) 2½" strip of each	¼ yd of each (2) 2½" strips of each
Fourth Dark	⅛ yd of each (1) 2½" strip of each	⅓ yd of each (3) 2½" strips of each
Fifth Dark	⅛ yd of each (1) 2½" strip of each	⅓ yd of each (3) 2½" strips of each
Optional Folded Border	¼ yd of each (4) 1¼" strips	⅓ yd (6) 1¼" strips
First Border	⅜ yd (4) 2½" strips	½ yd (6) 2½" strips
Second Border	⅔ yd (4) 4½" strips	1 yd (6) 5" strips
Binding	½ yd (4) 3" strips	⅔ yd (7) 3" strips
Backing	1¼ yds	3½ yds
Batting	40" x 40"	66" x 66"

Paste Your Fabric Here

Lap\Twin	Full/Queen	King
4 x 6 – 24 total 62" x 86"	6 x 6 = 36 total 88" x 88"	8 x 8 = 64 total 112" x 112"
¼ yd (2) 2½" strips	⅓ yd (3) 2½" strips	⅜ yd (4) 2½" strips
⅓ yd (3) 2½" strips	½ yd (5) 2½" strips	⅔ yd (8) 2½" strips
½ yd (5) 2½" strips	⅝ yd (7) 2½" strips	1 yd (12) 2½" strips
½ yd (6) 2½" strips	¾ yd (9) 2½" strips	1¼ yds (16) 2½" strips
⅔ yd (8) 2½" strips	1 yd (12) 2½" strips	1¾ yds (22) 2½" strips
⅛ yd of each (1) 2½" strip of each	¼ yd of each (2) 2½" strips of each	¼ yd of each (2) 2½" strips each
¼ yd of each (2) 2½" strips of each	⅓ yd of each (3) 2½" strips of each	½ yd of each (5) 2½" strips each
⅓ yd of each (3) 2½" strips of each	⅜ yd of each (4) 2½" strips of each	½ yd of each (6) 2½" strips each
⅓ yd of each (3) 2½" strips of each	½ yd of each (5) 2½" strips of each	⅔ yd of each (8) 2½" strips each
⅜ yd of each (4) 2½" strips of each	⅝ yd of each (7) 2½" strips of each	1 yd of each (11) 2½" strips each
⅜ yd of each (4) 2½" strips of each	⅝ yd of each (7) 2½" strips of each	1 yd of each (11) 2½" strips each
⅓ yd (6) 1¼" strips	½ yd (8) 1¼" strips	½ yd (10) 1¼" strips
½ yd (6) 2½" strips	⅔ yd (8) 2½" strips	¾ yd (10) 2½" strips
1¼ yds (7) 6" strips	1¾ yds (9) 6½" strips	2⅛ yds (11) 6½" strips
¾ yd (8) 3" strips	1 yd (9) 3" strips	1⅛ yds (12) 3" strips
4 yds	8 yds	10 yds
66" x 90"	96" x 96"	118" x 118"

Deciding Your Layout

1. Decide on layout for your size quilt. See page 25 for one layout, additional layouts on pages 13 and 24, or design your own log cabin layout.

2. Count number of blocks for Color Family One and Color Family Two.

Making Blocks

Work on one color family at a time.

1. Arrange your 2½" strips for First Color Family in sewing order. **Each fabric is used only once in the block.**

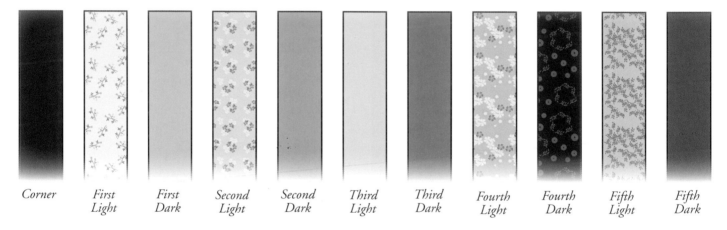

| Corner | First Light | First Dark | Second Light | Second Dark | Third Light | Third Dark | Fourth Light | Fourth Dark | Fifth Light | Fifth Dark |

2. Flip First Light strip right sides together to Corner strip, and sew.

3. Set seam with Light on top.

4. Open, and press seam toward Light. Seams are always pressed away from Corner.

5. Cut one 2½" section with Shape Cut™ or 6" x 12" ruler for each First Color Family block in your layout.

Adding First Dark

1. Stack patches wrong side up to left of First Dark strip.

2. Place patches right sides together to First Dark strip, and assembly-line sew.

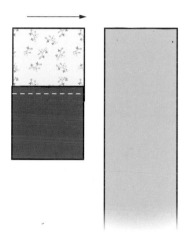

First Dark

3. With 6" Square Up ruler, cut strip even with block.

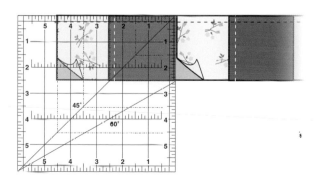

4. Set seam with First Dark on top.

5. Open, and press toward Dark.

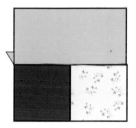

Adding Second Light

1. Stack patches wrong side up to left of Second Light strip, and assembly-line sew.

2. Cut strip even with blocks.

3. Set seam with Light on top, open, and press toward Light.

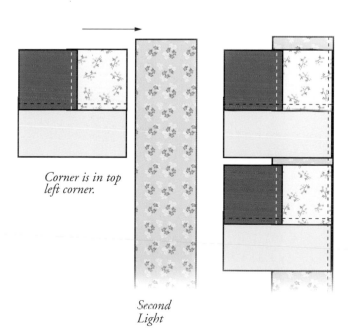

Corner is in top left corner.

Second Light

Adding Second Dark

1. Stack patches wrong side up to left of Second Dark strip.

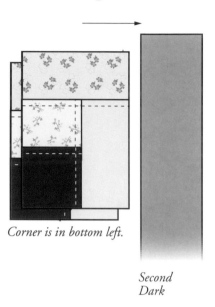

Corner is in bottom left.

*Second
Dark*

2. Assembly-line sew.

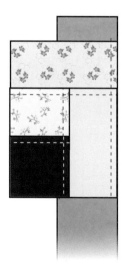

3. Cut strip even with blocks.

4. Set seams with Second Dark on top, open, and press toward Dark.

Adding Third Light

1. Stack patches wrong side up to left of Third Light strip.

Corner is in top left.

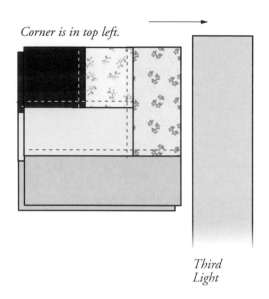

*Third
Light*

2. Assembly-line sew.

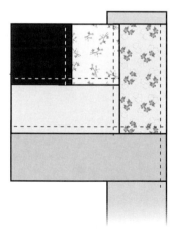

3. Cut strip even with blocks.

4. Set seam with Light on top, open, and press toward Light.

Adding Third Dark

1. Stack patches wrong side up to left of Third Dark strip.

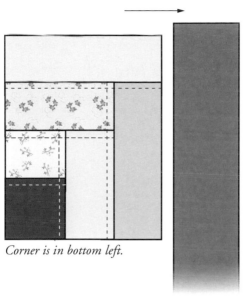

Corner is in bottom left.

Third Dark

2. Assembly-line sew.

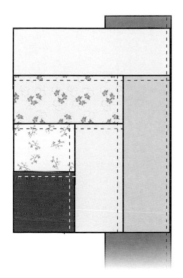

3. Cut strip even with blocks.

4. Set seam with Dark on top, open, and press toward Dark.

Adding Fourth Light

1. Stack patches wrong side up to left of Fourth Light strip.

Corner is in top left.

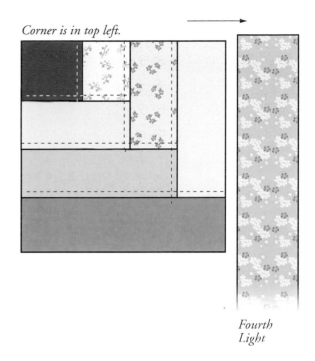

Fourth Light

2. Assembly-line sew.

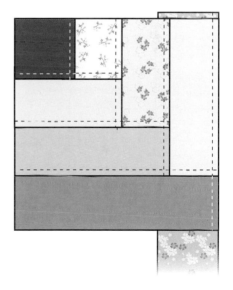

3. Cut strip even with blocks.

4. Set seam with Light on top, open, and press toward Light.

Adding Fourth Dark

1. Stack patches wrong side up to left of Fourth Dark strip.

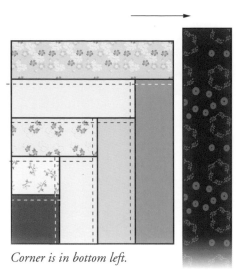

Corner is in bottom left.

Fourth Dark

2. Assembly-line sew.

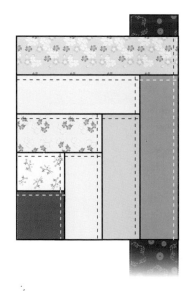

3. Cut strip even with blocks.

4. Set seam with Dark on top, open, and press toward Dark.

Adding Fifth Light

1. Stack patches wrong side up to left of Fifth Light strip.

Corner is in top left.

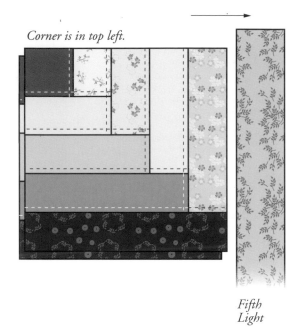

Fifth Light

2. Assembly-line sew.

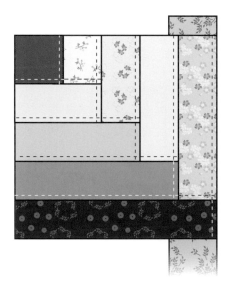

3. Cut strip even with blocks.

4. Set seam with Light on top, open, and press toward Light.

Adding Fifth Dark

1. Stack patches wrong side up to left of Fifth Dark strip.

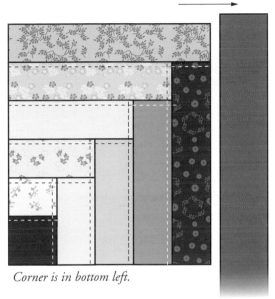

Corner is in bottom left.

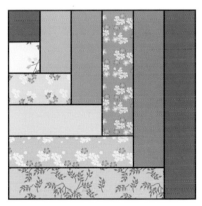

Fifth Dark

2. Assembly-line sew.

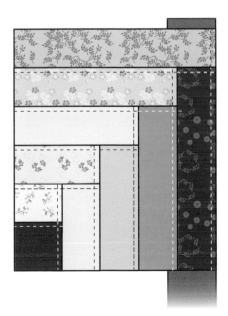

3. Cut strip even with blocks.

4. Set seam with Dark on top, open, and press toward Dark.

Squaring Up Block

1. Place 12½" Square Up ruler on block.

2. If necessary, straighten outside edges.

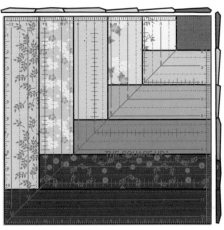

Color Family One

3. Repeat sewing process with Second Color Family.

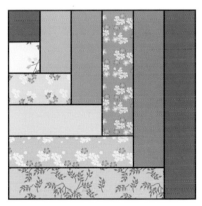

Color Family Two

Sewing Top Together

1. Lay out blocks in your selected layout.

2. Assembly-line sew vertical rows.

3. Sew remaining rows, pushing seams in opposite directions.

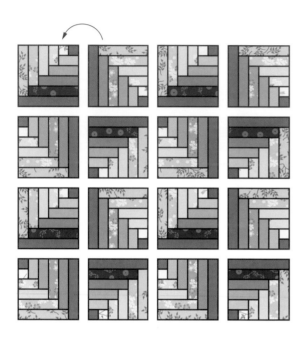

3. Place Folded Border on two opposite sides, matching raw edges. Sew ⅛" from raw edges with 10 stitches per inch or #3 setting. Trim even with sides of quilt top. **Do not fold out.**

4. Repeat on remaining two sides.

5. Turn to **Finishing Instructions** on page 226.

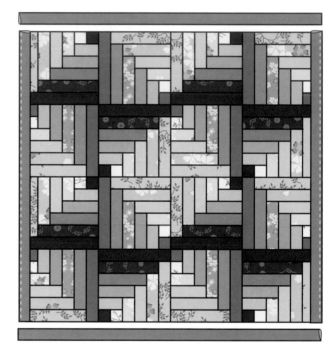

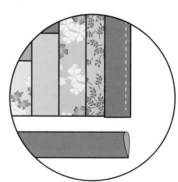

Making Optional Folded Border

1. Sew 1¼" strips into one long piece.

2. Press 1¼" strips in half lengthwise, wrong sides together.

	Red Block First Color Family	Green Block Second Color Family	Number of Blocks
Wallhanging	8	8	4 x 4
Lap/Twin	12	12	4 x 6
Full/Queen	16	20	6 x 6
King	28	36	8 x 8

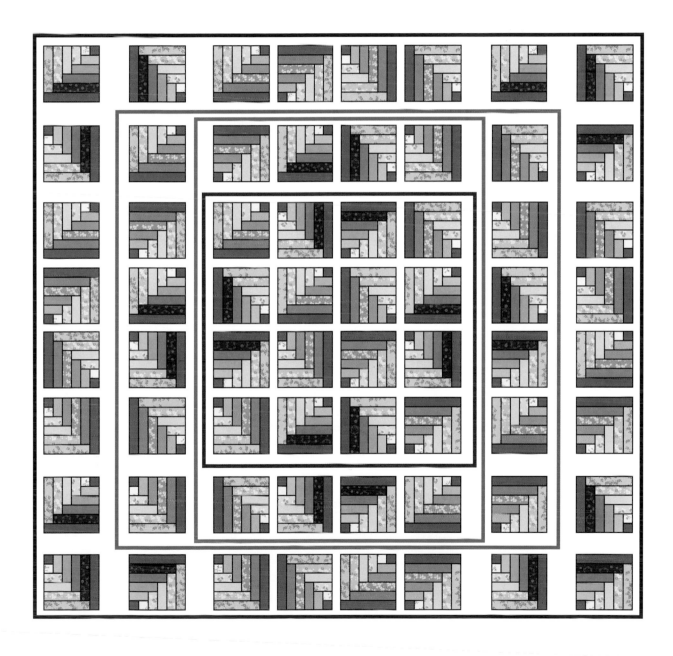

Love the Log Cabin Quilt

Two years later, in 1980, Bill broke my heart. He passed the bar and walked out the door, leaving me to raise the boys alone! We were devastated, but never tell a German girl she can't do anything without you. I took food stamps for three months, and used that time to set up an aggressive teaching schedule. We became experts at dumpster digging for class fabric. Orion once exclaimed as he looked over our evening haul, "Mommy, we must be the richest people on the block. Look at all our scraps!" It didn't take long before we loved the log cabin! It took us from the "scraps of life" to the top of the world. I'm proud of my sons and how we tied ourselves together.

Talented graphic artist Pam Nedlik redrew Bill's illustrations, and typeset the text, bringing our "home grown" Quilt in a Day book to its next level.

*Class at JoAnns
in Pittsburgh,
Pennsylvania*

Grant, El, and Orion

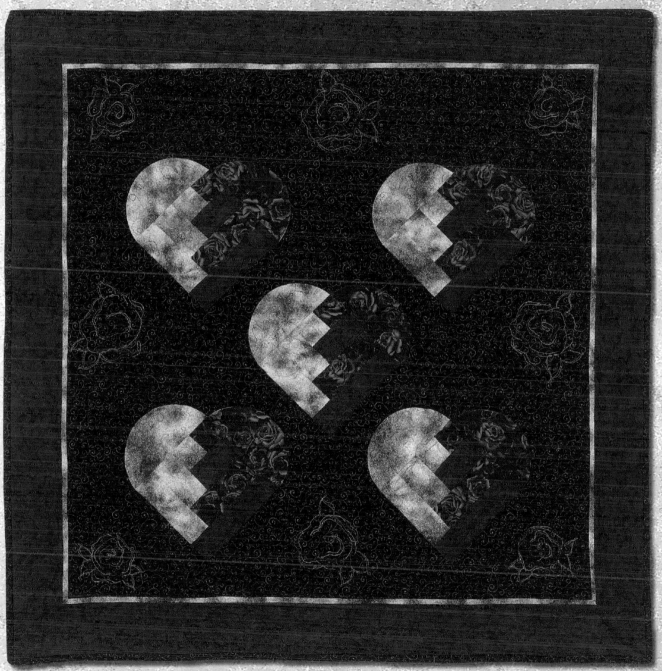

With a Victorian theme in mind, Marie poised her shades of pink hearts on a background of black and repeated the black for her lattice and cornerstones. She used variegated thread to quilt shadow roses in her "Hearts & Flowers" wall hanging design.

Pieced and Quilted by Marie Harper

50" x 50"

Fabric Selection

21" x 38"

For her two block table runner, Teresa chose rich, deep rose teamed with soft medium rose. Her hearts burst forth from the subdued backgrounds and are perfectly framed in deep rose.

Pieced and Quilted by Teresa Varnes

This lap robe warms the heart with its beauty and simplicity. Julie used several mediums, all in the same value, to achieve this soft, clean cut look.

53" x 72"

Pieced by Julia Markovitz
Quilted by Nancy Letchworth

With doves to grace the top of her heart, Teresa created a lovely one-block wallhanging with a folded border.

Pieced and Quilted by Teresa Varnes

24" x 24"

Fussy cut flowers adorn the cornerstones in Peggy's quilt, while deep and medium rose hearts are perfectly framed in petite roses. The beautiful effect is completed with the large scale rose border.

Pieced and Quilted Peggy Stinson

56" x 76"

Darkest
Heart Half Circle
First Border
Corner Square

350-87

Dark

Medium
Heart Half Circle

354-26

Background

352-07

Cornerstones
Fussy Cut
option

352-26

Lattice

355-70

Second Border

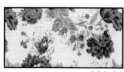

350-26

How to Select Your Fabric

For the blocks, select one medium appearing solid from a distance, or a small scale print. This fabric is repeated three times in the block, and is one of the Heart half circles. In addition, select a dark and darkest in similar value. These fabrics are repeated twice in the block. The darkest is the corner square and Heart half circle. Select a contrasting Background fabric in solid or large scale tone on tone print so Hearts stand out.

Cornerstones are attractive random or fussy cut. For fussy cut, select a 2" square design on your selected fabric, and count out the fussy cuts so you know how much fabric to purchase. Select a contrasting piece of fabric for the Lattice.

Yardage

	Finished Block Size 12" square	Pillow 16" x 16"	Wallhanging 24" x 24"
Paste Your Fabric Here	**Background** Heart Half Circle Side Triangles Corner Triangles	¼ yd (1) 4½" x 8½" (1) 4½" x 12½"	¼ yd (1) 4½" x 8½" (1) 4½" x 12½"
Paste Your Fabric Here	**Medium** Block Block Block Heart Half Circle Cornerstones	¼ yd (1) 2½" square (1) 2½" x 4½" (1) 2½" x 6½" (1) 4½" x 8½" (4) 2½" squares	¼ yd (1) 2½" square (1) 2½" x 4½" (1) 2½" x 6½" (1) 4½" x 8½"
Paste Your Fabric Here	**Dark** Block Block	⅛ yd (1) 2½" x 4½" (1) 2½" x 8½"	⅛ yd (1) 2½" x 4½" (1) 2½" x 8½"
Paste Your Fabric Here	**Darkest** Corner Block Heart Half Circle	¼ yd (1) 2½" square (1) 2½" x 6½" (1) 4½" x 8½"	¼ yd (1) 2½" square (1) 2½" x 6½" (1) 4½" x 8½"
Paste Your Fabric Here	**Second Medium** Lattice or Side Triangles and Corner Triangles	¼ yd (4) 2½" x 12½"	⅓ yd (2) 10½" squares
	Non-woven Fusible Interfacing	¼ yd (2) 4½" x 8½"	¼ yd (2) 4½" x 8½"
Paste Your Fabric Here	**Folded Border or First Border**		⅛ yd (2) 1¼" strips
Paste Your Fabric Here	**Second Border**		⅓ yd (3) 3½" strips
Paste Your Fabric Here	**Binding**		⅓ yd (3) 3" strips
	Backing	⅓ yd (2) 11" x 16½"	¾ yd
	Batting		28" x 28"
	Additional Supplies	18" Pillow Form 2 yds Piping or Lace	Dark Green Fabric Doves 3½" x 10½" piece Medium Green Fabric Wings 2½" x 6½" piece 10" Ribbon

Two Block Tablerunner	Five Block Wallhanging	Eight Block Lap Robe
21" x 37"	51" x 51"	56" x 76"

⅓ yd
   (2) 4½" x 8½"
   (2) 4½" x 12½"
	1½ yds
	   (3) 4½" strips cut into
	      (5) 4½" x 8½"
	      (5) 4½" x 12½"
	   (1) 22" square
	   (2) 14" squares
		1¾ yds
		   (5) 4½" strips cut into
		      (8) 4½" x 8½"
		      (8) 4½" x 12½"
		   (2) 22" squares
		   (2) 14" squares

¼ yd
   (2) 2½" squares
   (2) 2½" x 4½"
   (2) 2½" x 6½"
   (2) 4½" x 8½"
	½ yd
	   (3) 2½" strips
	   (2) 4½" strips cut into
	      (5) 4½" x 8½"
		⅔ yd
		   (4) 2½" strips
		   (2) 4½" strips cut into
		      (8) 4½" x 8½"

⅛ yd
   (2) 2½" x 4½"
   (2) 2½" x 8½"
	¼ yd
	   (2) 2½" strips
		⅓ yd
		   (3) 2½" strips

¼ yd
   (2) 2½" squares
   (2) 2½" x 6½"
   (2) 4½" x 8½"
	½ yd
	   (3) 2½" strips
	   (2) 4½" strips cut into
	      (5) 4½" x 8½"
		⅔ yd
		   (4) 2½" strips
		   (2) 4½" strips cut into
		      (8) 4½" x 8½"

⅝ yd
   (1) 18¼" square
   (2) 9½" squares
	½ yd
	   (6) 2½" strips
		⅔ yd
		   (8) 2½" strips

¼ yd
   (4) 4½" x 8½"
	⅔ yd
	   (10) 4½" x 8½"
		1 yd
		   (16) 4½" x 8½"

¼ yd
   (3) 2½" strips
	½ yd
	   (5) 1¼" strips or
	   (5) 2½" strips
		½ yd
		   (6) 1¼" strips or
		   (6) 2½" strips

	¾ yd
	   (5) 4½" strips
		1¼ yds
		   (7) 6" strips

⅓ yd
   (3) 3" strips
	½ yd
	   (5) 3" strips
		⅔ yd
		   (7) 3" strips

1⅛ yds	3¼ yds	4½ yds
24" x 40"	56" x 56"	62" x 82"

Making Blocks

1. Arrange 2½" strips in sewing order.

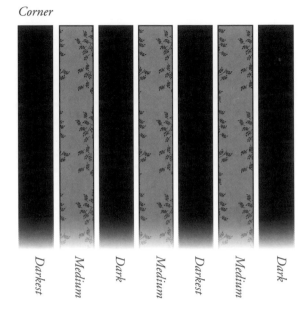

Corner

Darkest *Medium* *Dark* *Medium* *Darkest* *Medium* *Dark*

2. Cut one Medium strip and one Darkest strip in half. Flip Medium half strip right sides together to Darkest half strip, and sew.

3. Set seam with Medium on top, open, and press seam toward Medium. **Seams are always pressed away from Corner.**

Darkest   Medium

4. Cut into 2½" sections with Shape Cut™ or 6" x 12" ruler.

Five Block
Five

Eight Block
Eight

5. Stack patches wrong side up to left of Dark strip.

Strip is right side up.
Patches are wrong side up.

Dark

6. Place patches right sides together to Dark strip, and assembly-line sew.

7. Cut strip even with blocks.

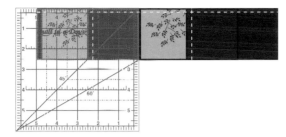

8. Set seam with Dark on top, open, and press toward Dark.

9. Stack patches wrong side up to left of second Medium strip, and assembly-line sew.

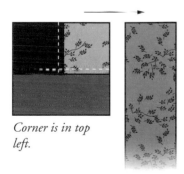

Corner is in top left.

Medium

10. Cut strip even with blocks.

11. Set seam with Medium on top, open, and press toward Medium.

12. Stack patches wrong side up to left of Darkest strip, and assembly-line sew.

Corner is in bottom left.

Darkest

13. Cut strip even with blocks.

14. Set seams with Darkest on top, open, and press toward Darkest.

15. Stack patches wrong side up to left of third Medium strip, and assembly-line sew.

Corner is in top left.

Medium

16. Cut strip even with blocks.

17. Set seam with Medium on top, open, and press toward Medium.

18. Stack patches wrong side up to left of Dark strip, and assembly-line sew.

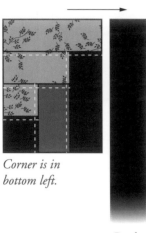

Corner is in bottom left.

Dark

19. Cut strip even with blocks.

20. Set seams with Dark on top, open, and press toward Dark.

21. Measure block. Block should be approximately 8½" square.

←———— 8½" ————→

Making Fusible Heart Half Circle

1. Trace half circle on smooth side of 4½" x 8½" rectangles of fusible interfacing with permanent marking pen. Pattern is on page 45. Trace two for each block.

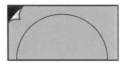

2. Place fusible, bumpy side of interfacing on right side of Medium and Darkest 4½" x 8½" rectangles.

3. Sew on line with 20 stitches per inch.

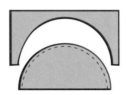

4. Trim to ⅛" away.

5. Turn right side out, and smooth curves.

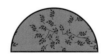

6. Place 4½" x 8½" Background rectangle next to block. Center Medium half circle on rectangle. Adjust so half circle is ¼" in from each side for seam allowance. Fuse in place with steam iron.

7. Sew rectangle to block.

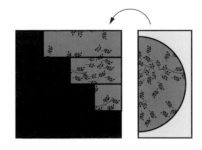

8. Press seam toward block.

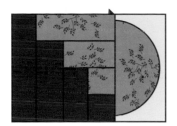

9. Place 4½" x 12½" Background rectangle next to block. Place Darkest half circle on rectangle, leaving ¼" seam on outside edge. Match inside edge of half circle to block.

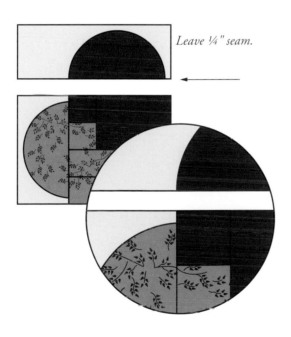

Leave ¼" seam.

10. Fuse Darkest half circle on rectangle.

11. Sew rectangle to block, matching heart.

12. Press seam toward block.

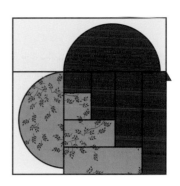

13. Stitch around top of heart with invisible thread and blind hem stitch.

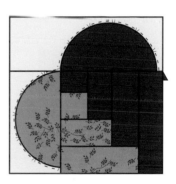

14. Measure block, approximately 12½".

15. Cut 2½" Lattice into strips same length as block.

Five Block
16

Eight Block
24

16. Cut 2½" medium strip into 2½" squares for Cornerstones.

Five Block
12

Eight Block
17

Sewing Lattice to Blocks

1. Count out two stacks of Lattice and one stack of Cornerstones with blocks.

   Five Block
   Five in each stack

   Eight Block
   Eight in each stack

2. Flip Lattice right sides together to block. Flip Cornerstone right sides together to Lattice.

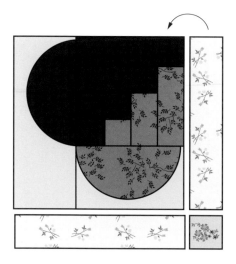

3. Assembly-line sew all pieces together.

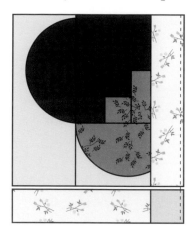

4. Clip threads after every Cornerstone.

5. Re-stack and assembly-line sew, pushing seams toward Lattice.

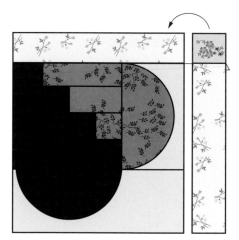

Press seams toward Lattice.

6. Clip threads holding blocks together.

Five Block
Clip after one block, and three blocks.

Eight Block
Clip after one block, three blocks, and three blocks.

Clip   *Clip*

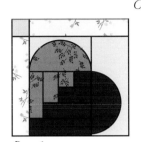
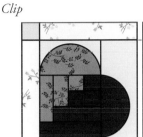
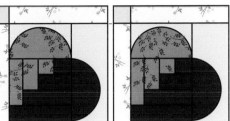

Row 1
Five Block example

Row 2

Row 3

7. Sew three chained blocks together into row. Press both seams up at Cornerstones.

Five Block
One Row

Eight Block
Two Rows

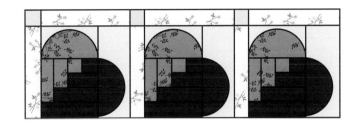

8. Stack remaining Lattice and Cornerstones, and assembly-line sew.

Five Block
Six Lattice and Seven Cornerstones

Eight Block
Seven Lattice and Eight Cornerstones

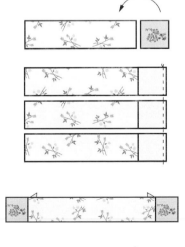

9. Sew last Cornerstone to opposite end of last Lattice.

10. Press seams toward Lattice.

11. Lay out diagonal rows in order.

12. Sew Lattice/Cornerstone to ends of rows.

13. Sew Cornerstone/Lattice/Cornerstone to end of last row.

14. Press seams toward Lattice.

Five Block Wallhanging

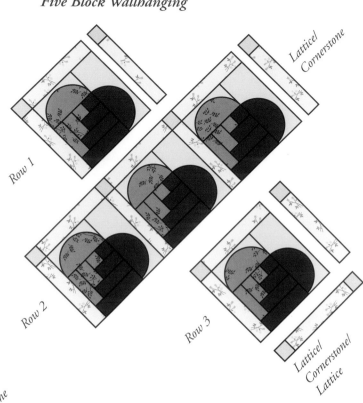

Eight Block Lap

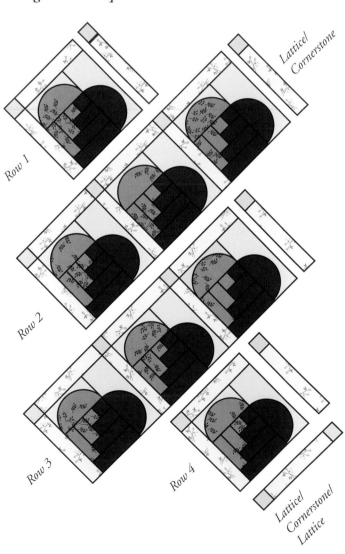

Cutting Side and Corner Triangles

1. Cut 22"
   squares for
   Side Triangles
   on both
   diagonals.

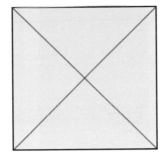

Five Block
Cut One

Eight Block
Cut Two

2. Sew Lattice/Cornerstone to
   Side Triangle.

Five Block
Sew One

Eight Block
Sew One

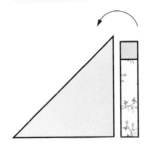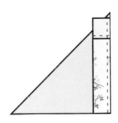

3. Sew second set in this order.

Five Block
Sew One

Eight Block
Sew Two

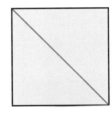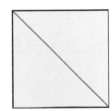

4. Press seams away from Side Triangle.

5. Cut two 14" squares in half on one
   diagonal for four corners of quilt.

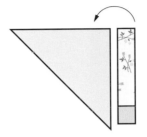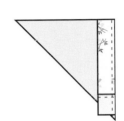

Laying Out Quilts

1. Lay out all pieces.

2. Flip Side Triangles right sides together
   to rows. Match and pin square edges. Let tip hang over. Sew with
   triangle on bottom.

3. Press seams away from Side Triangle. Square tips even with blocks.

4. Sew diagonal rows together, pressing seams toward Lattice.

5. Pin and sew Corner Triangles with triangle on bottom, and tips
   hanging out equally on each end. Square tips even with blocks.

6. Square outside edges ⅝" from Cornerstones for Optional Folded
   Border. Square outside edges ¼" from Cornerstones for regular
   Border.

Eight Block Lap

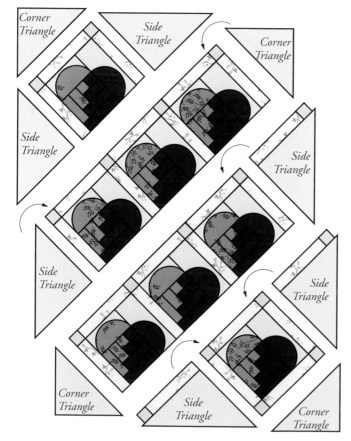

Five Block Wallhanging

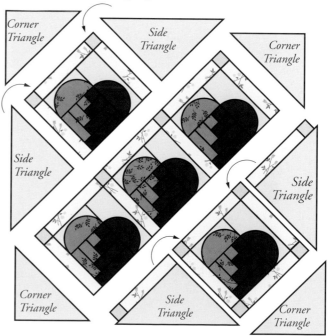

Making Optional Folded Border

1. Sew 1¼" strips into one long piece.

2. Press 1¼" strips in half lengthwise, wrong sides together.

3. Place Folded Border on two opposite sides, matching raw edges. Sew ⅛" from raw edges with 10 stitches per inch or #3 setting. Trim even with sides of quilt top. Do not fold out.

4. Repeat on remaining two sides.

5. Turn to **Finishing Instructions** on 226.

Heart Pillow

16" x 16"

1. Make one block following instructions on pages 32–35.

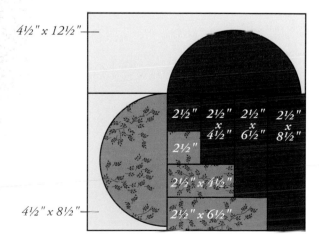

4½" x 12½"

2½" x 4½"   2½" x 6½"   2½" x 8½"

2½"

2½" x 4½"

4½" x 8½"

2½" x 6½"

2. Sew together with Lattice and Cornerstones.

3. Press seams toward Lattice.

4. Sew piping around outside edge.

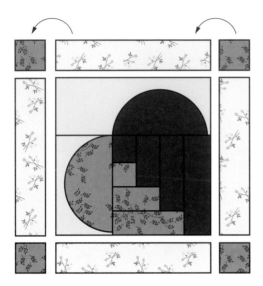

5. Hem one 16½" side on each Backing piece.

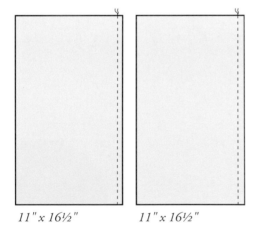

11" x 16½"   *11" x 16½"*

6. Overlap hemmed edges right sides together to pillow front.

7. Stitch around outside edge.

8. Turn right side out over pillow form.

One Block Wallhanging

1. Make one block following instructions on pages 32–35.

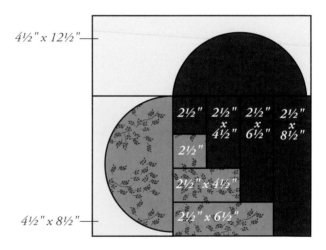

4½" x 12½"

4½" x 8½"

2½" x 4½"   2½" x 6½"   2½" x 8½"

2½"

2½" x 4½"

2½" x 6½"

2. Cut two 10½" squares in half on one diagonal.

3. Sew triangles to two opposite sides of block.

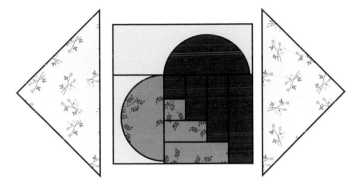

4. Set seams with triangles on top, open, and press seams toward triangles.

5. Trim tips even with block.

6. Center and sew triangles to two remaining sides.

7. Set seams with triangles on top, open, and press seams toward triangles.

8. Square ⅝" from outside edges for Folded Border.

9. Trace two Doves on smooth side of fusible interfacing, and sew. Patterns are on page 45. Applique instructions are on page 34.

10. Fuse in place with connecting ribbon. Sew around outside edges.

11. Press 1¼" strips in half lengthwise wrong sides together.

12. Place Folded Border on two opposite sides, matching raw edges. Sew ⅛" from raw edges with 10 stitches per inch or #3 setting. Trim even with sides of quilt top. Do not fold out.

13. Repeat on remaining two sides.

14. Turn to **Finishing Instructions** on page 226.

Two Block Tablerunner

1. Make two blocks following instructions on pages 32–35.

2. Cut 18¼" square on both diagonals for Side Triangles. Two triangles are extra.

3. Sew two triangles to two blocks. Press seams toward triangles. Trim tips even with blocks.

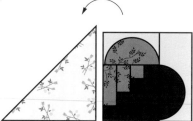

4. Sew blocks together.

5. Cut two 9½" squares on one diagonal.

6. Sew triangles to two opposite corners of tablerunner. Set seams with triangles on top, open, and press seams toward triangles. Trim tips even with block.

7. Sew two remaining triangles.

8. Square outside edges.

9. Sew Borders to tablerunner. Press seams toward Border.

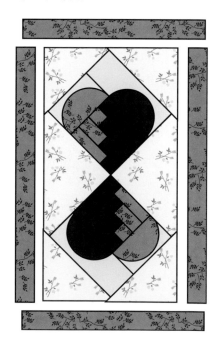

10. Turn to **Finishing Instructions** on page 226.

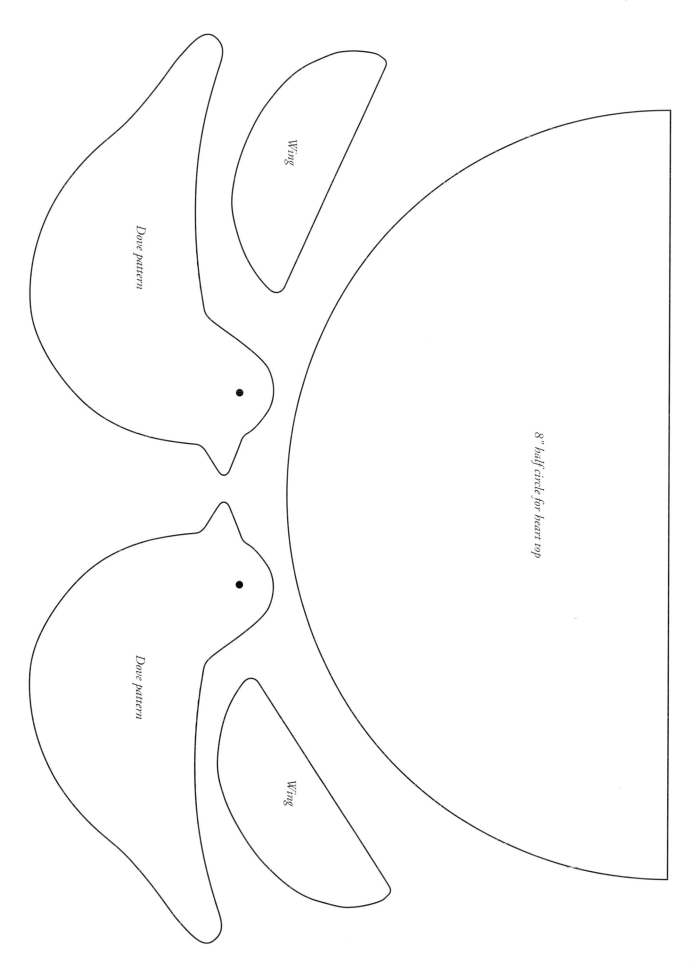

Dove pattern

Wing

8" half circle for heart top

Dove pattern

Wing

Four Sisters Quilt

In 1982, "baby sister" Judy flew in from Pennsylvania as back-up Mom while I traveled the country, teaching and inspiring students with Quilt in a Day techniques. Judy joined good friend and assistant Jeri Priestly Packard. In three days, Jeri had Judy in my garage packing quantity orders of Quilt in a Day books on Orion's discarded changing table. Times have changed! A long way from the original table, Judy continues to manage our shipping department, with her staff shipping out an excess of a quarter of a million books a year!

Middle sister Patricia was the artist for our next books, *Trio of Treasured Quilts* (1983), *Lover's Knot* (1985), and *Irish Chain* (1986). A trained professional, Patty is a master at putting together beautiful fabrics for quilts. After finishing the *Irish Chain*, Patty also took to the road, teaching Quilt in a Day techniques to thousands. Judy and I tease Patty that she can't stand to be away from us – she moved onto the same street as me! Maybe it's the other way around.

Oldest sister Kathy never did take up quilting. Perhaps it's just as well, having three obsessed with it. Kathy always rallied around our successes, and cheered us on!

And then there was Bruce…

Good friend Nancy Loftis knows my family well, and could not leave Bruce out. Just as my mom lined up all five of us for photos, Nancy lined up five dark squares in a row, and turned the blocks in a "fields and furrows" setting. Nancy's beautiful quilt showcases my second line of fabric, Rainbow Florals.

Pieced by Nancy Loftis
Quilted by Debra Jenks

54" x 74"

Fabric Selection

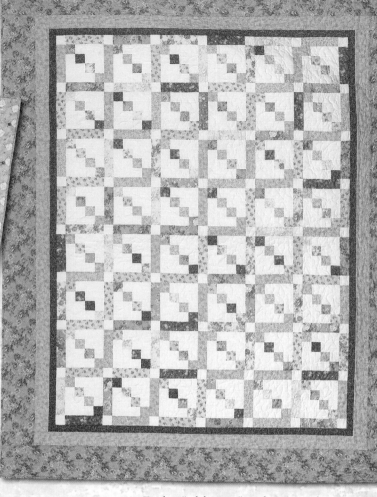

Nancy's approach to a scrappy quilt is softened by her use of the light tan background allowing a subtle effect for her pastel chains. Her borders are subdued in pastel prints resulting in a warm and cozy lap robe.

Pieced and
Quilted by
Nancy Letchworth
52" x 72"

For her "celebration" quilt, Nancy chose a scrappy look and used a palette of Yours Truly fabrics in pastels shades, set against a soft, white background. She cut her strips in quarters for variety. The Remembrance floral-print final border in light blue and pink compliments her deep green and bright pink borders.

Pieced by Nancy Loftis
Quilted by Debra Jenks
84" x 102"

For a masculine lap robe, Judy chose a tan background with shades of brown to grace her chains. Her use of bold black for the first border, followed by a multi-shaded brown border, make her quilt fit for a king!

Pieced by Judy Callahan
Quilted by Nancy Letchworth
52" x 72"

Yours Truly
Fabrics by
BENARTEX
INCORPORATED

Fabric A

350-44

Fabric B

354-26

Fabric C

354-40

Fabric D
First Border

350-87

Fabric E

352-49

Second Border

350-26

Background

354-39

With a beautiful floral frame, Sue made her planned quilt a stand out. She used red, caramel and green Yours Truly fabrics to create her lap robe in perfect harmony.

Pieced by Sue Bouchard
Quilted by Amie Potter
52" x 72"

How to Select Your Fabric

Select five different medium to dark fabrics that coordinate in various scales of prints as large scale, medium scale, small scale, and tone on tone. Fat quarters can be used for Fabrics A-D in smaller size quilts; just cut twice as many for half strips. Scrappy blocks can also be made with each half strip a different fabric.

Select one Background in tone on tone or solid from a distance that pulls all fabrics together.

Yardage

Finished Block Size 10" square	Wallhanging 3 x 3 = 9 total 43" x 43"	Lap 4 x 6 = 24 total 54" x 74"
Fabric A	⅛ yd (1) 2½" x 24" strip Represents half strip*	¼ yd (2) 2½" strips Cut in half You only need (3) half strips
Fabric B	⅛ yd (1) 2½" x 24" strip Represents half strip*	¼ yd (2) 2½" strips Cut in half You only need (3) half strips
Fabric C	⅛ yd (1) 2½" x 24" strip Represents half strip*	¼ yd (2) 2½" strips Cut in half You only need (3) half strips
Fabric D	⅛ yd (1) 2½" x 24" strip Represents half strip*	¼ yd (2) 2½" strips Cut in half You only need (3) half strips
Fabric E	⅝ yds (3) 2½" strips (1) 8½" strip Cut in half	1¼ yds (5) 2½" strips (3) 8½" strips Cut in half
Background	1 yd (6) 2½" strips Cut (2) 2½" x 24" Cut (1) in half (1) 4½" x 24" strip Represents half strip* (1) 6½" x 24" strip Represents half strip*	2 yds (13) 2½" strips Cut (3) in half (2) 4½" strips Cut in half (2) 6½" strips Cut in half
First Border	⅓ yd (4) 2" strips	⅝ yd (7) 2½" strips
Second Border	⅝ yd (4) 4½" strips	1⅛ yds (7) 5" strips
Third Border		
Binding	½ yd (5) 3" strips	⅔ yd (7) 3" strips
Backing	3 yds	4½ yds
Batting	50" x 50"	60" x 80"

Paste Your Fabric Here

*Half strips approximately 21" long are perfect for all size quilts because they are divisible by eight, or 8 x 2½"=20". The exception is the Wallhanging with nine blocks, or 9 x 2½"=22½". To save time sewing, cut Wallhanging strips at 24" in length to represent a half strip. The remaining part of the Wallhanging strip is not needed.

Twin	Full/Queen	King
4 x 8 = 32 total 68" x 108"	6 x 8 = 48 total 88" x 108"	8 x 8 = 64 total 108" x 108"
¼ yd (2) 2½" strips Cut in half	⅓ yd (3) 2½" strips Cut in half	⅜ yd (4) 2½" strips Cut in half
¼ yd (2) 2½" strips Cut in half	⅓ yd (3) 2½" strips Cut in half	⅜ yd (4) 2½" strips Cut in half
¼ yd (2) 2½" strips Cut in half	⅓ yd (3) 2½" strips Cut in half	⅜ yd (4) 2½" strips Cut in half
¼ yd (2) 2½" strips Cut in half	⅓ yd (3) 2½" strips Cut in half	⅜ yd (4) 2½" strips Cut in half
1½ yds (7) 2½" strips (3) 8½" strips Cut in half	2¼ yds (10) 2½" strips (4) 8½" strips Cut in half	2⅔ yds (13) 2½" strips (5) 8½" strips Cut in half
2 yds (18) 2½" strips Cut (5) in half (2) 4½" strips Cut in half (2) 6½" strips Cut in half	3 yds (25) 2½" strips Cut (7) in half (3) 4½" strips Cut in half (3) 6½" strips Cut in half	3¾ yds (32) 2½" strips Cut (9) in half (4) 4½" strips Cut in half (4) 6½" strips Cut in half
⅝ yd (7) 2½" strips	1 yd (8) 2½" strips	1 yd (9) 2½" strips
1⅛ yds (7) 5" strips	1⅓ yds (9) 5" strips	1⅓ yds (9) 5" strips
2 yds (9) 7" strips	2⅛ yds (10) 7" strips	2½ yds (11) 7" strips
⅞ yd (9) 3" strips	1 yd (10) 3" strips	1 yd (11) 3" strips
6½ yds	9½ yds	9½ yds
74" x 112"	92" x 112"	112" x 112"

Making Four-Patches

Use an accurate ¼" seam and 15 stitches per inch, or 2.0 setting on computerized machine. Sew and measure width of two 2½" strips. They should be 4½" wide.

1. Count out and sew 2½" half strips Fabric A and 2½" half strips Background right sides together.

4. Count out and sew 2½" half strips Fabric B and 2½" half strips Background right sides together.

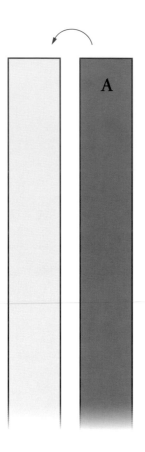

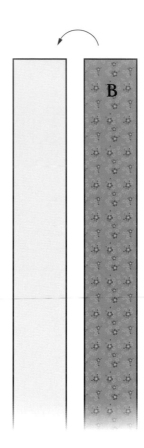

Half Strips Each	
Wallhanging	1
Lap	3
Twin	4
Full/Queen	6
King	8

Half Strips Each	
Wallhanging	1
Lap	3
Twin	4
Full/Queen	6
King	8

2. Set seams with Fabric A on top.

3. Open, and press toward Fabric A.

5. Set seams with Fabric B on top.

6. Open, and press toward Fabric B.

7. Place Fabric A strip right side up on gridded cutting mat with Background across top. Place Fabric B strip right sides together to it with Fabric B across top. Lock seams. Line up strips with grid.

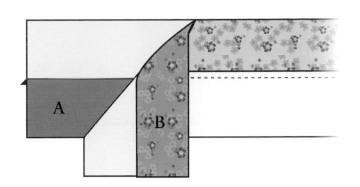

8. Square left end. Cut 2½" pairs. Stack on spare ruler to carry to sewing area.

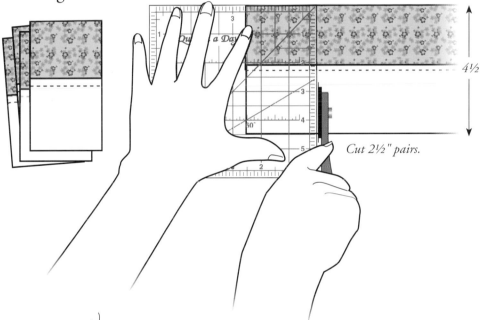

4½"

Cut 2½" pairs.

9. Matching outside edges and center seam, assembly-line sew. Use stiletto to hold outside edges together and seams flat.

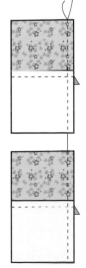

Number of 2½" Pairs	
Wallhanging	9
Lap	24
Twin	32
Full/Queen	48
King	64

10. At center seam, unsew the three stitches indicated in red with stiletto or seam ripper.

11. Turn block over, and repeat removing red stitches at center.

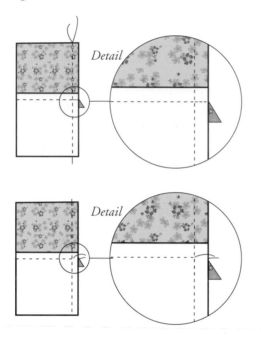

Detail

Detail

Adding First Round

1. Stack 2½" Background strips right side up with patch. Place Fabric B in upper left corner.

2. Flip patch right sides together to Background, and assembly-line sew.

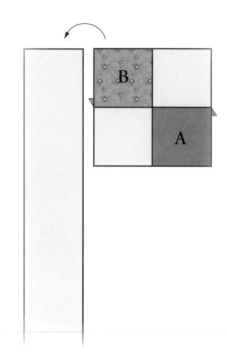

B

A

12. Open center seams and push down flat to form a tiny Four-Patch. Press.

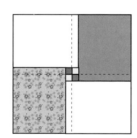

13. Measure. Size should be 4½".

3. Set seams with Background on top, open, and press toward Background.

4. Cut Background strip even with patches.

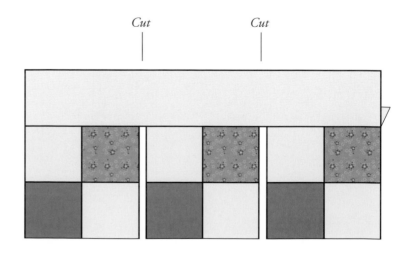

Cut   *Cut*

5. Sew 2½" half strips Fabric C right sides together with 4½" half strips Background.

Half Strips Each	
Wallhanging	1
Lap	3
Twin	4
Full/Queen	6
King	8

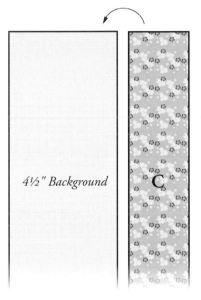

If your Four-Patch is less than 4½", sliver trim 4½" Background strip to that measurement.

4½" Background   C

6. Set seams with Background on top, open, and **press toward Background.**

7. Cut into 2½" segments.

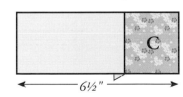

C

— 6½" —

Number of 2½" Segments	
Wallhanging	9
Lap	24
Twin	32
Full/Queen	48
King	64

8. Stack Four-Patches with Fabric C segments.

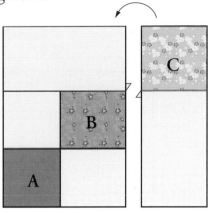

C

B

A

9. Flip right sides together, lock seams, and assembly-line sew.

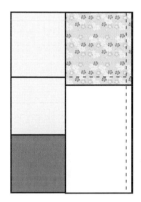

10. Set seams with Background/Fabric C on top. Open, and press against seam. If necessary, trim extra.

11. **Measure. A/B/C Patch should be 6½".**

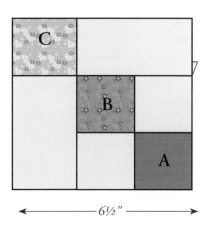

C

B

A

— 6½" —

Adding Second Round

1. Stack 2½" Background strips right side up with patches. Turn patches with Fabric C in upper left corner.

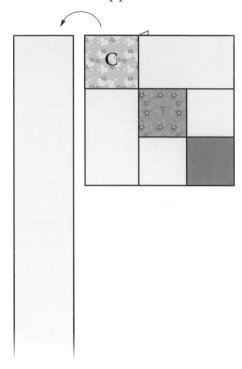

2. Flip patches right sides together to Background, and assembly-line sew.

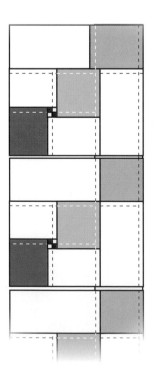

3. Set seams with Background on top, open, and press toward Background.

4. Cut apart between patches.

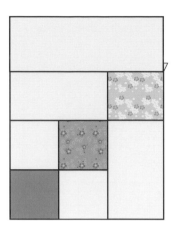

5. Sew 2½" half strips Fabric D right sides together with 6½" half Background strips.

Half Strips Each	
Wallhanging	1
Lap	3
Twin	4
Full/Queen	6
King	8

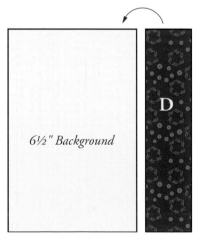

6½" Background

If your A/B/C Patch is less than 6½", sliver trim Background to that measurement.

6. Set seams with Background on top, open, and press toward Background.

7. Cut into 2½" segments.

Number of 2½" Segments	
Wallhanging	9
Lap	24
Twin	32
Full/Queen	48
King	64

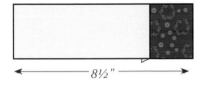

8. Stack patches with Fabric D segments.

9. Flip right sides together, lock seams, and assembly-line sew.

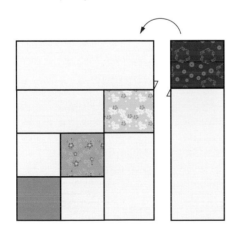

10. Set seams with Background/Fabric D on top.

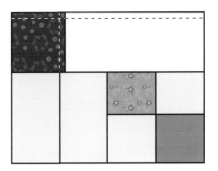

11. Open, and press toward Background.

12. Measure. A/B/C/D Patch should be 8½".

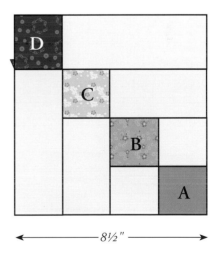

Adding Third Round

1. Stack 2½" Fabric E strips right side up with patches. Turn patches with Fabric D in upper left corner.

2. Flip patches right sides together to Fabric E, and assembly-line sew.

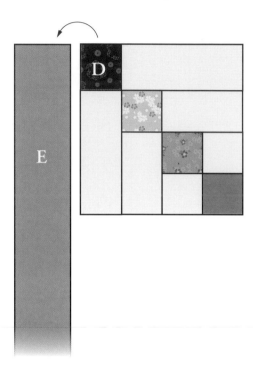

5. Sew 2½" Background half strips right sides together with 8½" Fabric E half strips.

6. Set seams with Fabric E on top, open, and press toward Fabric E.

Half Strips Each	
Wallhanging	2
Lap	5
Twin	6
Full/Queen	8
King	10

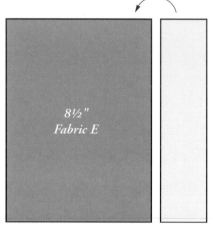

If your A/B/C/D Patch is less than 8½", sliver trim Fabric E to that measurement.

3. Set seams with Fabric E on top, open, and press toward Fabric E.

4. Cut apart between patches.

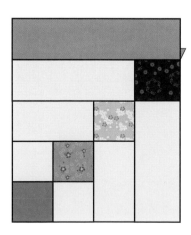

7. Cut into 2½" segments. *(Save extras for bottom row.)*

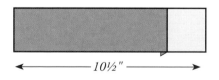

←——— 10½" ———→

Number of Segments	
Wallhanging	15
Lap	34
Twin	44
Full/Queen	62
King	80

8. Stack patches with Fabric F segments.

9. Flip right sides together, lock seams, and assembly-line sew.

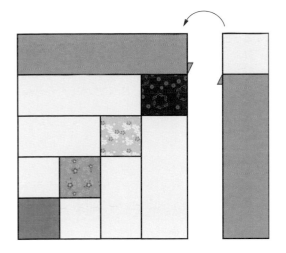

Sewing Wallhanging Together

For larger quilts, turn to page 60.

1. Divide blocks into a stack of six and a stack of three.

2. Press last seam in stack of six toward Fabric E/Background.

4. Lay out stack of six blocks in first and third vertical rows.

5. Lay out stack of three in middle vertical row.

6. Sew blocks together into rows.

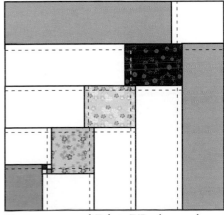

Six seams toward Fabric E/Background

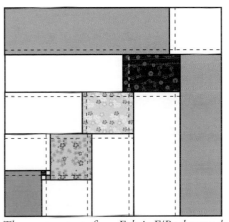

Three seams away from Fabric E/Background

3. Press last seam in stack of three away from Fabric E/Background.

Sewing Larger Quilts Together

1. Divide blocks into two equal stacks.

2. In first stack, press last seam toward Fabric E/ Background.

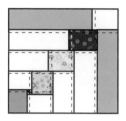

Seams toward Fabric E/Background

3. In second stack, press last seam away from Fabric E/ Background.

4. Sliver trim edges if necessary.

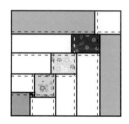

Seams away from Fabric E/Background

Sliver trim edges if necessary.

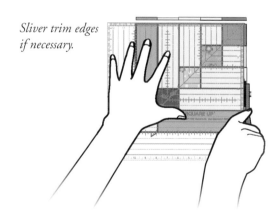

5. Assembly-line sew two stacks of blocks together into pairs, locking seams.

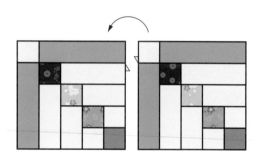

6. Assembly-line sew pairs of blocks together into rows. See pages 62 and 63 for layouts.

	Blocks in Rows	Rows
Lap	4	6
Twin	4	8
Full/Queen	6	8
King	8	8

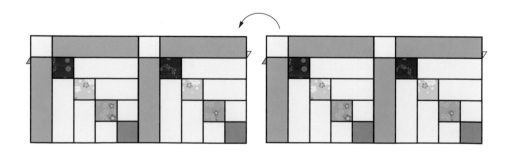

Sewing Outside and Bottom Rows

1. Sew remaining 2½" Fabric E/
   Backgound pieces to ends of rows.

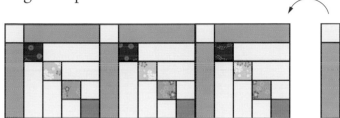

2. Sew rows together.

3. Cut one 2½" Background square.

4. Assembly-line sew remaining 2½"
   Fabric E/Background pieces and 2½"
   Background square together.

5. Sew Fabric E row to bottom of quilt.

6. Turn to **Finishing Instructions** on
   page 226.

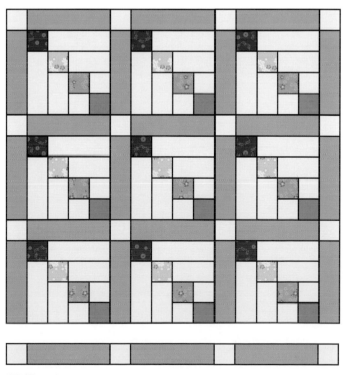

Wallhanging

Layouts

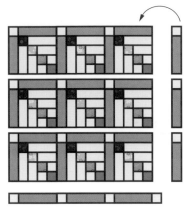

Wallhanging

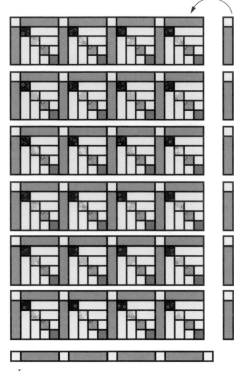

Lap

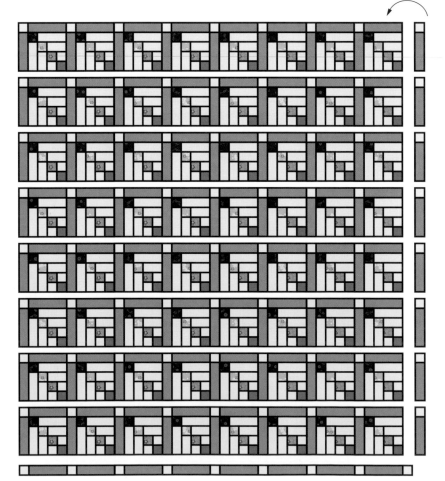

King

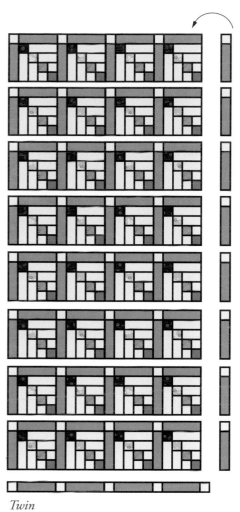

Twin

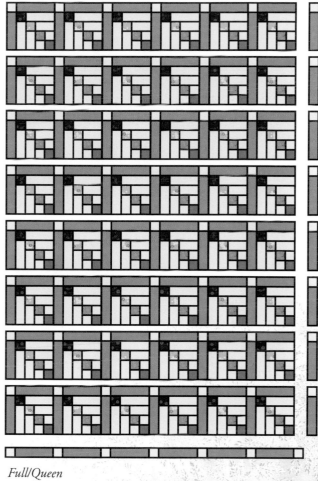

Full/Queen

Pieced by Teresa Varnes
Quilted by Peggy Stinson
43" x 43"

Nine-Patch Party Quilt

The party really started when we moved to 1955 Diamond Street, San Marcos, California in 1983. To celebrate, we covered the building with a 576 block log cabin quilt, our attempt at the world's largest quilt. We didn't receive that recognition, but we sure had fun trying!

Jeri Packard moved in the orders – and bills! Patty moved in 50 bolts of fabric from my bedroom, Judy moved in a couple hundred books, and I was in business! Judy Peterson, first store employee, served customers daily, and every other Saturday. We delighted when average daily sales reached $50. Barbara Bredeweg, our first teacher, thrilled students with how to "cut through 14 layers of fabric before you say shazam."

Ten years later, I purchased the 16,000 square foot building, and it's been a suitable home for Quilt in a Day ever since. Today it houses thirty employees, serving customers, students, and visitors from around the world.

Patricia Knoechel

Judy Peterson

Barbara Bredeweg

Fabric Selection

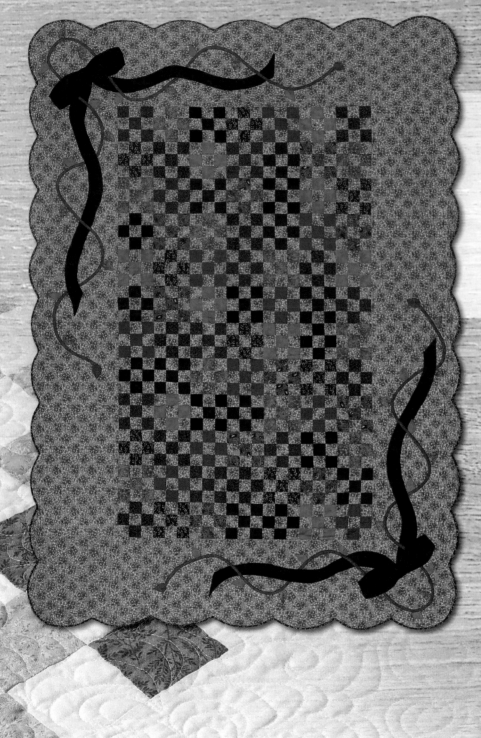

For a lush fall cast, Peggy selected rich jewel box tones and tan background fabric. She carried the background fabric out to the borders, complimented the quilt with an appliquéd red ribbon, and intertwined appliquéd greenery as the finishing touch.

*Pieced and Quilted by
Peggy Stinson
68" x 98"*

Yours Truly
Fabrics by
BENARTEX
INCORPORATED

Print 1

352-60

Print 2

355-26

Print 3
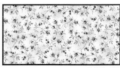
355-40

Print 4

352-84

Print 5
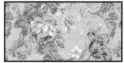
350-01

Print 6

354-84

Print 7

356-05

Print 8

355-01

Background

352-07

Using "Floral Garden" in tone on tone cream as her background and border, the mood of Sue's quilt is soft and light. Her appliquéd blossoms echo the "Yours Truly" fabrics of the Nine-Patches to complete the decorative corners.

Pieced and Quilted by Sue Bouchard
34" x 34"

How to Select Your Fabric

Select a variety of small scale floral prints, or 1930's reproduction feed sack prints. To compliment the prints, select one Background in a good quality muslin or natural colored cotton.

This is a perfect project to use fat eighth or fat quarter prints. Just cut them up into 8" squares! Use their leftovers for appliquéd flowers and leaves.

Yardage

*Each set of Background and Print 8" squares makes one positive Nine-Patch with five dark squares and one negative Nine-Patch with four dark squares.

Finished Block Size 6" square	Wallhanging 4 x 4= 16 total 36" x 36"	Lap 6 x 8 = 48 total 48" x 60"

Background Blocks
 	
Border
	1½ yds
	   (2) 8" strips cut into
	      (8) 8" squares
	   (4) 7" strips
		2½ yds
		   (5) 8" strips cut into
		      (24) 8" squares
		   (6) 7" strips

Prints Blocks
Flowers
	(8) ¼ yd pieces
	   (1) 8" square from each
	   (1) 4" x 8" from each
		(12) ¼ yd pieces
		   (2) 8" squares from each
		   (1) 4" x 8" from each

Green for Leaves	⅛ yd (3) 4" x 8" pieces	¼ yd (5) 4" x 8" pieces
Non-Woven Fusible Interfacing Flowers Leaves	¾ yd (8) 4" x 8" pieces (3) 4" x 8" pieces	1 yd (12) 4" x 8" pieces (5) 4" x 8" pieces
100% Cotton Batting for Stuffing Applique	¼ yd	¼ yd

Bias Binding	½ yd cut into
	   (1) 16" strip
		1 yd cut into
		   (2) 16" strips

Backing	1¼ yds	3 yds
Batting	42" x 42"	54" x 68"

Paste Your Fabric Here

Twin	Full/Queen	King
7 x 12 = 84 total 70" x 100"	11 x 14 = 154 total 92" x 116"	14 x 14 = 196 total 116" x 116"
5 yds 　(9) 8" strips cut into 　　(42) 8" squares 　(7) 16" strips	**9¼ yds** 　(16) 8" strips cut into 　　(77) 8" squares 　(11) 16" strips	**10½ yds** 　(20) 8" strips cut into 　　(98) 8" squares 　(12) 16" strips
(14) ¼ yd pieces 　(3) 8" squares from each 　(1) 4" x 8" from each	**(16) ⅜ yd pieces** 　(5) 8" squares from each 　(1) 4" x 8" from each	**(20) ⅜ yd pieces** 　(5) 8" squares from each 　(1) 4" x 8" from each
⅓ yd (6) 4" x 8" pieces	**⅓ yd** (6) 4" x 8" pieces	**⅓ yd** (8) 4" x 8" pieces
1¼ yds (14) 4" x 8" pieces (6) 4" x 8" pieces	**1⅓ yds** (16) 4" x 8" pieces (6) 4" x 8" pieces	**1½ yds** (20) 4" x 8" pieces (8) 4" x 8" pieces
¼ yd	**¼ yd**	**¼ yd**
1 yd cut into 　(2) 16" strips	**1½ yds cut into** 　(3) 16" strips	**1½ yds cut into** 　(3) 16" strips
6½ yds	**9 yds**	**10 yds**
80" x 110"	104" x 122"	122" x 122"

Making Positive and Negative Nine-Patch Blocks

Each set of 8" squares makes one positive and one negative block.

1. Place one 8" Background square right sides together to one 8" print square. Match grains. Pin.

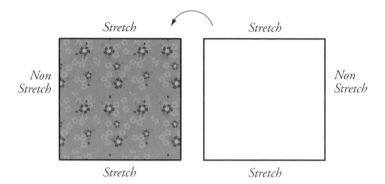

Number of Sets	
Wallhanging	8
Lap	24
Twin	42
Full/Queen	77
King	98

2. Assembly-line sew two opposite edges with ¼" seam and 15 stitches per inch, or 2.0 on computerized machine.

3. Set seams.

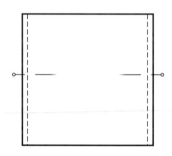

4. With 6" x 12" ruler, cut 2½" strip from one side. Measure from raw edge.

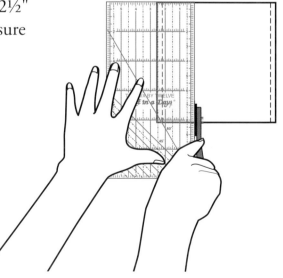

5. Turn piece and cut second 2½" strip from raw edge.

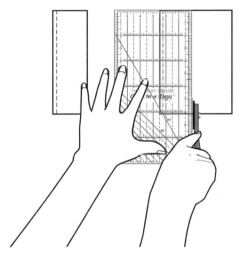

7. Set seams of paired strips with Print on top.

8. Open, and press toward Print.

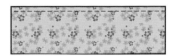

9. Sew single 2½" strips to paired strips.

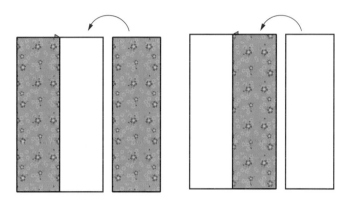

6. Layer cut center section into 2½" single strips.

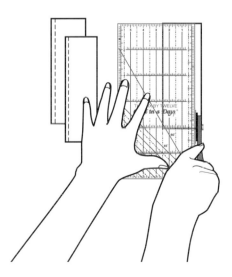

10. Set seams with Print on top.

11. Open, and press toward Print.

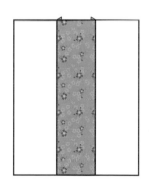

12. Place strip sets right sides together, locking seams.

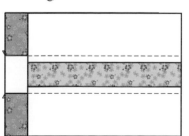

13. Sliver trim ends to straighten. Pin.

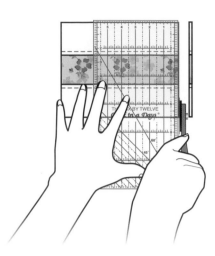

15. Cut 2½" strips from opposite sides, measuring from raw edges.

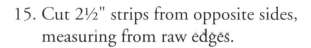

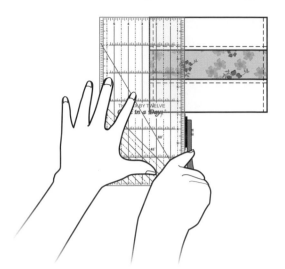

14. Sew two opposite sides with ¼" seams.

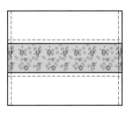

16. Layer cut center section into 2½" strips.

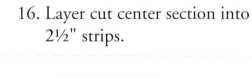

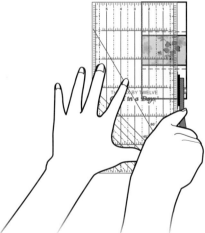

17. Set seams with two dark squares on top, open and press.

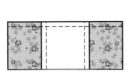 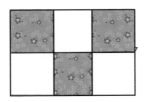

19. Sew together with locking seams.

 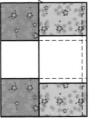 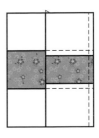

18. Lay out pieces to make positive and negative blocks.

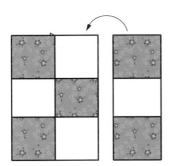 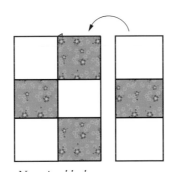

Positive block   *Negative blocks*

20. Press two sets of blocks differently so seams lock when sewing blocks together.

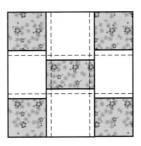 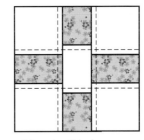

Positive Blocks

Press final seams away from center, toward sections with two Prints.

Negative Blocks

Press final seams toward center, or section with two Prints.

21. Place in two separate stacks.

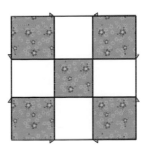 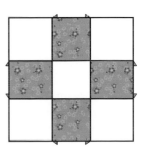

Sewing Top Together

1. Lay out blocks alternating between positive and negative blocks.

2. Assembly-line sew vertical rows together.

3. Sew remaining rows, locking seams in opposite directions.

4. Sew borders to four sides.

Rows Across and Down	
Wallhanging	4 x 4
Lap	6 x 8
Twin	7 x 12
Full/Queen	11 x 14
King	14 x 14

Wallhanging and Lap:
Sew 7" Borders to all sides.

Twin, Full/Queen, King:
Sew 16" Borders to all sides.

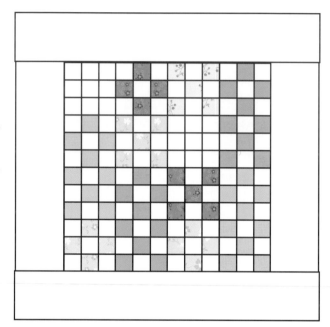

5. Layer quilt top with backing and batting.

6. Mark diagonal quilting lines with Hera marker through every Background square, or every other Background square.

7. Safety pin layers together away from quilting lines.

8. Quilt on lines with walking foot and 10 stitches per inch.

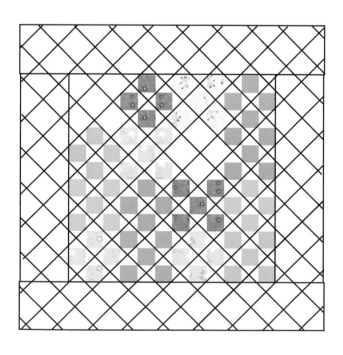

Marking Scallop Border

1. Select appropriate scallop pattern on page 83 and trace on template plastic. Cut out template.

2. Mark diagonal lines with Hera marker on corners if diagonal line not quilted.

3. Place corner of scallop template on diagonal line. Trace with marking pen.

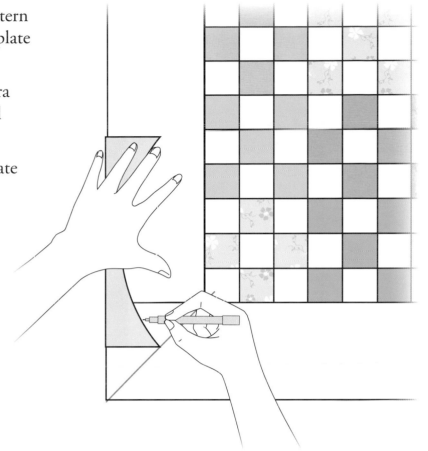

4. Mark scallops from two ends toward middle. Make adjustment in very center scallop to fit. You may need to elongate scallops or shorten.

5. Staystitch on scallop line.

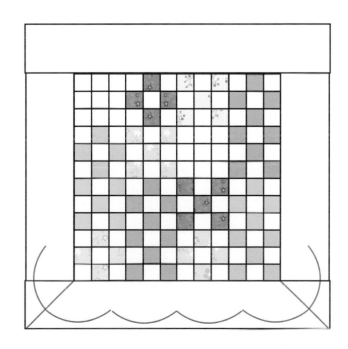

Making Bias Binding

1. Cut binding fabric into 16" selvage to selvage strips.

2. Line up 45° line on 6" x 24" ruler with left edge of 16" strip.

3. Cut on diagonal. Fabric to left of cut can also be used for binding.

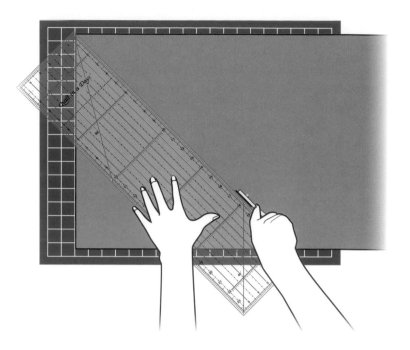

4. Move ruler over 2" from diagonal cut. Cut again.

5. Cut 16" strip into required number of 2" bias strips.

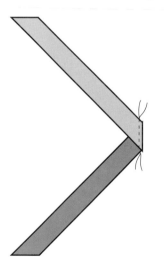

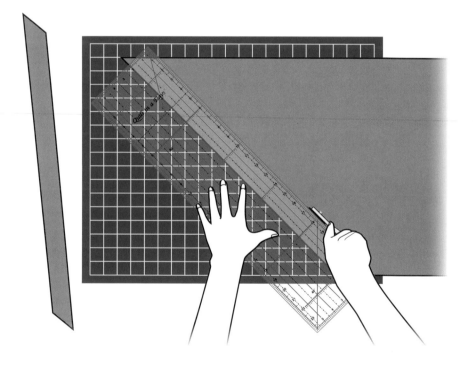

6. Piece bias strips together on angle to approximate length for your size quilt.

	Number of Strips	Length of Bias Strip
Wallhanging	7	161"
Lap	14	332"
Twin	17	391"
Full/Queen	22	506"
King	24	552"

7. Press diagonal seams open.

8. Press bias strip in half lengthwise wrong sides together.

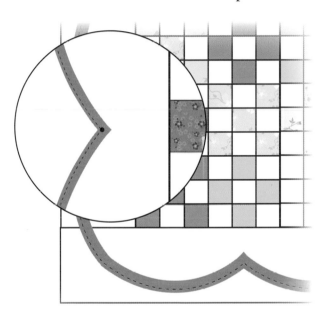

9. Line up raw edge of binding with marked scallop line. Leave 3" of binding loose. Begin stitching scant ¼" seam in middle of scallop.

10. Stitch to point between two scallops. Stop with needle in fabric.

11. Raise presser foot, pivot quilt, lower presser foot, and continue stitching around quilt, **easing binding around curves.**

12. Stop stitching 4" from where ends will overlap.

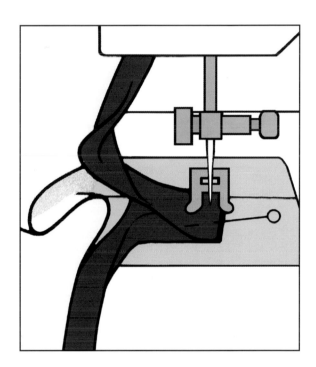

13. Open up folded ends and pin right sides together. Sew a ¼" seam.

14. Continue stitching binding in place.

15. Trim quilt top even with binding. Clip between scallops to seam.

16. Turn binding to back side. Pull folded edge over stitching line. Inside corners will automatically fold in place. Hand stitch folded edge.

Making Flowers and Leaves

1. Trace patterns on template plastic with template marking pen. Cut out shapes. Patterns are on page 83.

2. Turn 4" x 8" non-woven fusible interfacing smooth side up. With permanent marking pen, trace two flowers on smooth side of interfacing with ½" space between each. Trace twenty-two leaves, or as many as you wish, on smooth side of interfacing.

3. Place rough, fusible side of interfacing against right side of 4" x 8" fabrics for flowers. Pin. Place traced leaves against right side of green fabric.

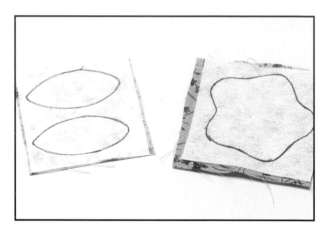

4. With 20 stitches per inch or 1.8 on computerized machines, sew on drawn lines.

5. Trim seams to ⅛". Clip inside curves.

6. Cut small opening in center of interfacing. Insert straw into hole. Push straw against fabric.

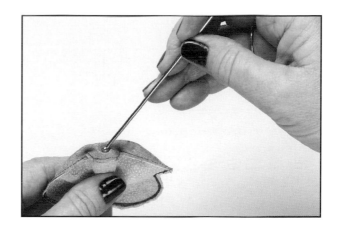

7. Place ball of ball point bodkin on fabric stretched over straw. Gently push fabric into straw with bodkin to start turning piece.

8. Remove straw and bodkin. Insert straw in second half, and turn right side out. Run bodkin around inside edge, pushing out seams.

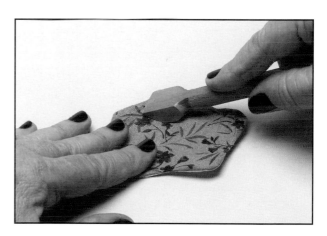

9. From right side, push fabric over interfacing edge with wooden iron.

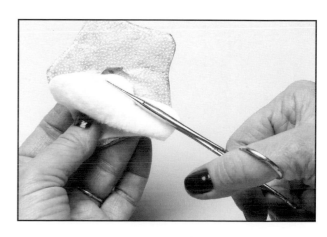

10. Cut 100% cotton batting same size as flower. Insert batting though opening with hemostat.

11. Arrange applique pieces on corner, steam press in place, and hand or machine stitch around outside edges. Stitch buttons to centers of flowers.

Night Glow

*This is the perfect quilt for fat quarters! Just cut 8"
squares for the Nine-Patch
blocks, and then chop up
the remaining fabric into 3"
strips for the binding and
1¼" strips for the Folded
Border. Waste not, want not!*

Pieced by Eleanor Burns
Quilted by Sandy Thompson
38" x 47"

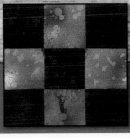

Yardage

Finished Block Size 6" square	Wallhanging 4 x 5 = 20 total 38" x 47"
Background	**1¾ yds**
Paste Your Fabric Here	**Blocks**
	(2) 8" strips cut into
	(10) 8" squares
	Side Triangles
	(1) 10" strip cut into
	(4) 10" squares
	Cut on both diagonals
	Corners
	(2) 6" squares
	Cut on one diagonal
	Solid Squares
	(2) 6½" strips cut into
	(12) 6½" squares
	Border
	(4) 4½" strips
Brights	**(5) ¼ yd pieces**
Paste Your Fabric Here	Cut from each piece
	Blocks
Paste Your Fabric Here	(2) 8" squares
	Pieced Binding
Paste Your Fabric Here	(2) 3" strips x length of fabric
	Pieced Folded Border
Paste Your Fabric Here	(1-2) 1¼" strips x length of fabric
Paste Your Fabric Here	
Backing	**1½ yds**
Paste Your Fabric Here	
Batting	**44" x 52"**

Making Top

1. Make ten sets of positive and negative Nine-Patch blocks from 8" squares. Follow directions on pages 70 – 73.

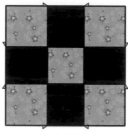
Positive

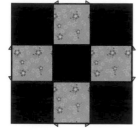
Negative

2. Place six negative blocks in center of layout on point, and four in corners.

3. Place remaining ten positive blocks around outside edge.

4. Place twelve 6½" Solid Squares, and Side Triangles in layout. Sew together in diagonal rows. Sew four Corners last.

5. Square outside edges.

6. Piece 1¼" Folded Border strips into four strips same length as 4½" Border strips

7. Press Folded Border, wrong sides together, and sew to individual Border strips.

8. Sew Border to sides and then to top and bottom.

9. Piece 3" Binding strips into approximate length of 180".

10. Turn to **Finishing Instructions** on pages 226.

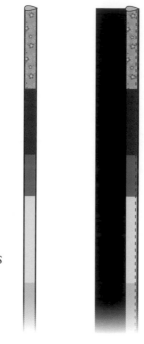

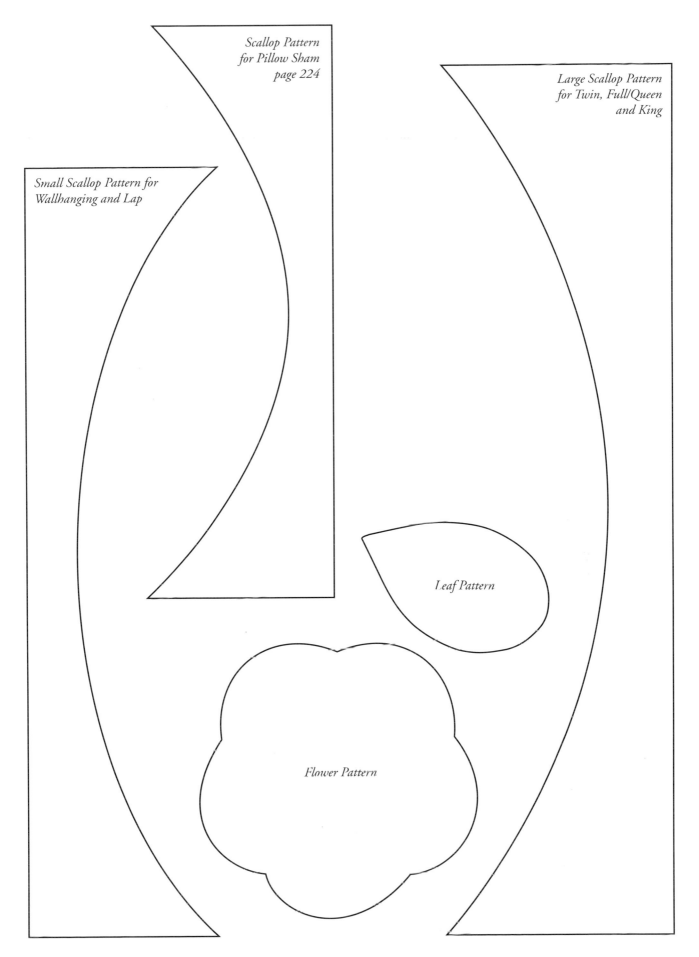

Scallop Pattern
for Pillow Sham
page 224

Large Scallop Pattern
for Twin, Full/Queen
and King

Small Scallop Pattern for
Wallhanging and Lap

Leaf Pattern

Flower Pattern

Nine-Patch and Stripe

Grant, El and Orion

Meet the Burns' team - three parallel stripes side by side, forming one tight unit!

Grant and Orion were always ready to get the job done! Their after school responsibilities included addressing class flyers and sorting by zip code. Already industrious paperboys, they took extra flyers and delivered them in the neighborhood. They packed mail orders that piled up through the day. Boxes of Quilt in a Day books constantly arriving from the printer needed to by shelved. They were quite excited when we advanced from a plain old ladder to a forklift! Orion became a close up camera man at a young age.

Grant and friend

Grant, El and Orion

El and Orion

Fabric Selection

These quilts are unique because positive and negative nine-patch and stripe blocks are made at the same time for both quilts. In the first quilt, negative nine-patches with four dark red squares and positive stripes with two green rails are set together with medium scale print side and corner triangles. The pieced border has two green rails and one background rail.

The second quilt is the exact opposite featuring positive nine-patch blocks with five dark red squares, and negative stripes with one green rail. The large scale print used for the setting contrasts with the background. The pieced border has two background rails and one green rail.

First Quilt
Pieced by Sue Bouchard
Quilted by Neta Virgin
69" x 102"

Yours Truly
Fabrics by

BENARTEX
INCORPORATED

Second Quilt
Pieced by Sue Bouchard
Quilted by Neta Virgin
69" x 102"

Light
Background
for both Quilts

Pieced Border

352-07

Stripe Block
for both Quilts

Pieced Border

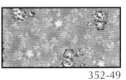

352-49

Nine-Patches
for both Quilts

Pieced Border

354-26

Setting for
First Quilt

352-26

Setting for
Second Quilt

350-26

How to Select Your Fabric

Select one light background, one dark for the nine-patches, and one medium dark for the stripes. Yardage is enough for blocks in both quilts.

The remaining fabric is selected in sets of two, so the two quilts can coordinate together, or look entirely different. For first quilt, select a setting fabric that contrasts or blends with the stripe fabric. For the second quilt, select a setting fabric that contrasts with the background.

Wallhanging and Lap do not have pieced borders.

Yardage

	Finished Block Size 6" square	Wallhanging 12 Nine-Patch 16 Stripe for each 53" x 53"	Lap 17 Nine-Patch 24 Stripe for each 57" x 74"
Yardage for Blocks of Both Quilts	**Background** Nine-Patch/Stripe *Enough for both Quilts*	1½ yds (6) 8" strips cut into (28) 8" squares	2¼ yds (9) 8" strips cut into (41) 8" squares
	Nine-Patches *Enough for both Quilts*	1 yd (3) 8" strips cut into (12) 8" squares	1 yd (4) 8" strips cut into (17) 8" squares
	Stripe Block *Enough for both Quilts*	1 yd (4) 8" strips cut into (16) 8" squares	1¼ yds (5) 8" strips cut into (24) 8" squares
Yardage for Finishing of Specific Quilts	**Light Setting for Quilt One** Solid Squares	1 yd (1) 6½" strip cut into (5) 6½" squares	1 yd (2) 6½" strips cut into (8) 6½" squares
	Side Triangles Corner Triangles	(1) 19" square (2) 15" squares	(2) 19" squares (2) 15" squares
	Medium Setting for Quilt Two Solid Squares	1 yd (1) 6½" strip cut into (5) 6½" squares	1 yd (2) 6½" strips cut into (8) 6½" squares
	Side Triangles Corner Triangles	(1) 19" square (2) 15" squares	(2) 19" squares (2) 15" squares
	First Border *Purchase for each Quilt*	½ yd (5) 2½" strips	½ yd (6) 2½" strips
	Pieced Border *Purchase for each Quilt* Single Stripe Double Stripe		
	Last Border *Purchase for each Quilt*	¾ yd (6) 4" strips	1⅜ yds (7) 6" strips
	Binding *Purchase for each Quilt*	⅝ yd (6) 3" strips	⅔ yd (7) 3" strips
	Backing *Purchase for each Quilt*	3⅓ yds	3½ yds
	Batting *Purchase for each Quilt*	58" x 58"	63" x 80"

Paste Your Fabric Here

	Twin	Full/Queen	King
	26 Nine-Patch 32 Stripe for each 69" x 102"	**35 Nine-Patch 48 Stripe for each 94" x 108"**	**44 Nine-Patch 64 Stripe for each 108" x 108"**
	2¾ yds (12) 8" strips cut into (58) 8" squares	4 yds (17) 8" strips cut into (83) 8" squares	5 yds (22) 8" strips cut into (108) 8" squares
	1½ yds (6) 8" strips cut into (26) 8" squares	1¾ yds (7) 8" strips cut into (35) 8" squares	2¼ yds (9) 8" strips cut into (44) 8" squares
	1¾ yds (7) 8" strips cut into (32) 8" squares	2½ yds (10) 8" strips cut into (48) 8" squares	3 yds (13) 8" strips cut into (64) 8" squares

	Twin	Full/Queen	King
	2 yds (2) 6½" strips cut into (11) 6½" squares (3) 19" squares (2) 15" squares	2¼ yds (3) 6½" strips cut into (18) 6½" squares (3) 19" squares (2) 15" squares	2¾ yds (5) 6½" strips cut into (25) 6½" squares (3) 19" squares (2) 15" squares
	2 yds (2) 6½" strips cut into (11) 6½" squares (3) 19" squares (2) 15" squares	2¼ yds (3) 6½" strips cut into (18) 6½" squares (3) 19" squares (2) 15" squares	2¼ yds (5) 6½" strips cut into (25) 6½" squares (3) 19" squares (2) 15" squares
	⅔ yd (7) 2½" strips	1 yd (8) 3½" strips	1 yd (8) 3½" strips
	⅔ yd (7) 2½" strips 1⅛ yds (14) 2½" strips	⅔ yd (8) 2½" strips 1¼ yds (16) 2½" strips	¾ yd (9) 2½" strips 1½ yds (18) 2½" strips
	1¾ yds (9) 6" strips	2¾ yds (11) 8½" strips	2¾ yds (11) 8½" strips
	⅞ yd (9) 3" strips	1 yd (11) 3" strips	1⅛ yds (12) 3" strips
	6 yds	8½ yds	10 yds
	75" x 108"	102" x 116"	116" x 116"

Making Nine-Patch and Stripe Blocks

With these instructions, there are enough blocks for two quilts.

1. Place 8" Background strips right sides together to 8" Nine-Patch strips, and 8" Stripe strips. You can use partial strips.

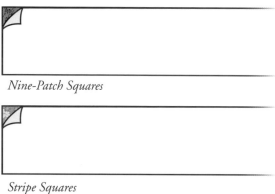

Nine-Patch Squares

Stripe Squares

2. Layer cut 8" squares. Pin sides.

	Nine-Patch Sets	Stripe Sets
Wallhanging	12	16
Lap	17	24
Twin	26	32
Full/Queen	35	48
King	44	64

3. Assembly-line sew two opposite edges with ¼" seam and 15 stitches per inch, or 2.0 on computerized machine.

4. Set seams.

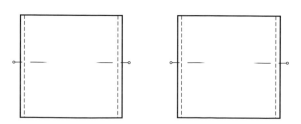

5. With 6" x 12" ruler, cut 2½" strip from one side. Measure from raw edge.

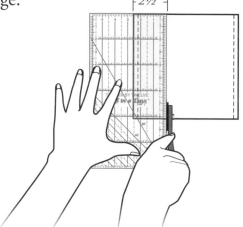

6. Turn piece and cut second 2½" strip from raw edge.

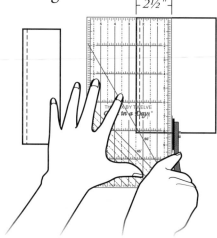

7. Layer cut center section into 2½" single strips.

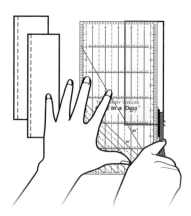

8. Set seams of paired strips with print on top.

9. Open, and press toward print.

10. Sew single 2½" strips to paired strips.

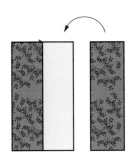

Nine-Patch Strips

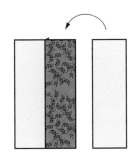

Stripe Strips

11. Set seams with print on top.

12. Open, and press toward print. Continue sewing Nine-Patch blocks on page 92.

 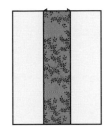

Positive stripe   *Negative stripe*

13. Separate out Stripe blocks for both quilts and set aside.

First Quilt	
Wallhanging	16
Lap	24
Twin	32
Full/Queen	48
King	64

Positive block

Second Quilt	
Wallhanging	16
Lap	24
Twin	32
Full/Queen	48
King	64

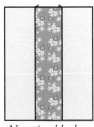

Negative block

Finishing Nine-Patch Blocks

1. Place strip sets right sides together, locking seams.

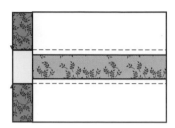

2. Sliver trim ends to straighten. Pin.

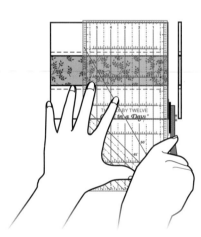

3. Sew two opposite sides with ¼" seams.

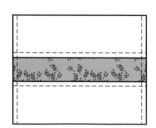

4. Cut 2½" strips from opposite sides, measuring from raw edges.

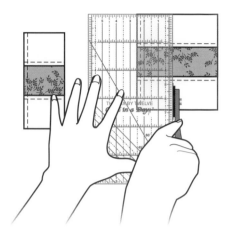

5. Layer cut center section into 2½" strips. Separate cut pieces.

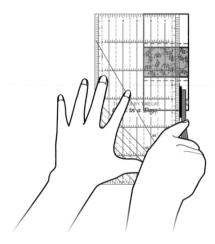

6. Set seams with two dark squares on top, open and press.

7. Lay out positive and negative blocks.

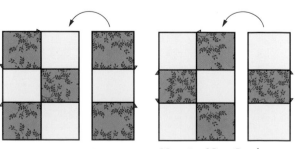

Positive Nine-Patch   *Negative Nine-Patch*

8. Sew together with locking seams.

9. Press two sets of blocks differently so seams lock when sewing blocks together.

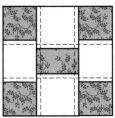 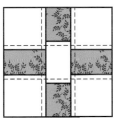

Positive Blocks
Press final seams away from center, toward sections with two prints.

Negative Blocks
Press final seams toward center, or section with two prints.

10. Place in two separate stacks. Four blocks are Border Corners on Twin, Full/Queen, and King.

First Quilt	
Wallhanging	12
Lap	17
Twin	26
Full/Queen	35
King	44

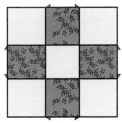

Negative block

Second Quilt	
Wallhanging	12
Lap	17
Twin	26
Full/Queen	35
King	44

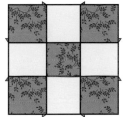

Positive block

11. Measure Nine-Patch blocks. Square Stripe blocks to same measurement.

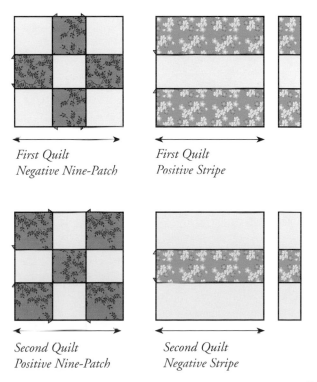

First Quilt
Negative Nine-Patch

First Quilt
Positive Stripe

Second Quilt
Positive Nine-Patch

Second Quilt
Negative Stripe

Sewing Tops Together

1. Separate blocks for two quilts.

2. Cut 19" squares for Side Triangles on both diagonals.

3. Cut 15" squares for Corner Triangles on one diagonal.

4. If necessary, trim 6½" Solid Squares to same size as Nine-Patch and Stripe blocks.

5. Lay out blocks in your size. Illustrations are for Second Quilt. First Quilt is laid out the same.

6. Sew Nine-Patch and Stripe rows together. If needed, add third row.

7. Sew rows in opposite direction. Press seams toward Nine-Patch and away from Stripe.

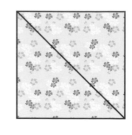

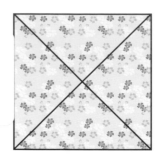

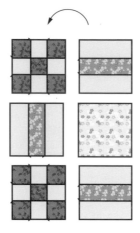

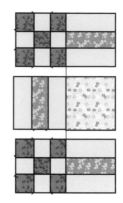

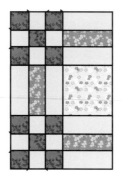

Wallhanging

Lap

Twin

8. **Lap, Twin and Full/Queen:**
Sew one Nine-Patch to one Stripe for Lap and Full/Queen. Sew two Nine-Patch to two Stripe for Twin. Press seam toward Nine-Patch.

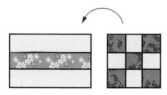

9. Sew patches to Side Triangle and press seam toward Triangle.

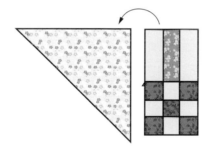

10. Sew Side Triangles to ends of rows. Press seams toward Triangles. Trim tips.

11. Sew rows together. Sew Corners last.

12. Press and square outside edges, leaving ¼" seams.

13. Add First Border.

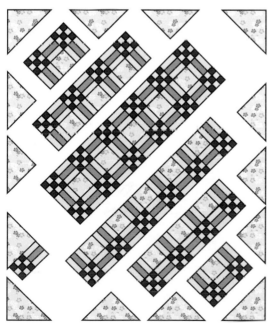

Full/Queen

King

Making a Pieced Border

Wallhanging and Lap do not have a pieced border.

1. Sew 2½" strips into three long pieces.

2. Sew three 2½" strips together lengthwise.

3. Press seams toward darkest fabric.

4. Measure sides, top, and bottom of quilt.

5. Cut two stripes same length as sides and two stripes same length as top and bottom.

6. Pin and sew stripes to sides.

7. Press seams toward stripes.

8. Sew Nine-Patch to both ends of top and bottom stripes.

9. Press seams toward stripes.

10. Pin and sew stripes to top and bottom.

11. Press seams toward stripes.

12. Turn to **Finishing Instructions** on page 226.

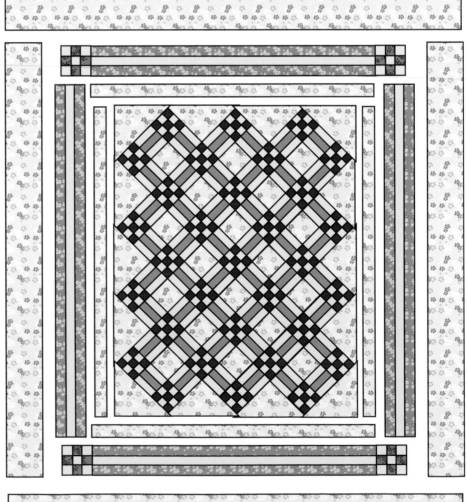

Scrappy Nine-Patches and Stripes

What a fantastic way to use up fat quarter bundles!

Working solely with reds, greens, and caramels from Eleanor's Yours Truly fabric line, Sue Bouchard masterfully stitched up these two companion scrappy quilts. She cut a variety of 8" background squares paired with cheery red and green squares to match the number of blocks indicated on the yardage chart. To make each quilt look unique, she set one together with the same background, and the other with scrappy green side and corner triangles. Plain borders beautifully accent the center blocks.

Top Quilt
Pieced by Sue Bouchard
Quilted by Sandy Thompson

Bottom Quilt
Pieced by Sue Bouchard
Quilted by Amie Potter

Both quilts are 57" x 74"

Road to Stardom Quilt

In 1987 intern Kendra Heipt persevered with a pilot Quilt in a Day program until she secured us a weekly spot on The Learning Channel. Then we really had to scramble to buy equipment and put programs in the can! Public Broadcasting Systems (PBS) and Good Life Cable Network followed.

When viewers express amazement at how perfect my patches match, I always remind them of editing. They ask, "why does it take you only a half hour to make a quilt," followed by "Who picks up the fabric?"

Presently, we have recorded twenty-four series with over 266 half hour programs.

Our crew is small, at times working with only two cameramen, doubling talents as floor director, and tape operator. On shoots like those, we pad the credits with sound operator Tabitha Burns, talented grandpuppy, who loves to lounge about the set.

One of my favorites is the Bears in the Woods series, shot on location at Ashley Lake, Montana. Assistant Sue Bouchard, decked in her father's waders, stood by with cue cards on the Flying Geese segment. Director Brian Steutel pulled it together, despite the less than state of the art studio.

Fabric Selection

Teresa chose "Rainbow Florals" in deep purple, green and navy blue to give her wallhanging a striking, rich effect. Her stars are brilliant against a soft yellow background.

Pieced and Quilted by Teresa Varnes
64" x 64"

In a scrappy mosaic of creams and tan background, Eleanor's stars appear to surge from her flannel quilt. She cut pieces from a huge stack of fall fat quarters until she had the total number of background squares. Each Star is from a different fabric. El chose complimentary burnt red as a frame and echoed her star fabrics in the border for a beautiful quilt, fit for a queen!

Pieced by Eleanor Burns
Quilted by Carol Selepec
96" x 96"

Yours Truly
Fabrics by

INCORPORATED

Stars
First Border

350-87

Background

352-07

Chain

350-44

Four-Patches
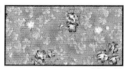
354-26

Four-Patches

352-49

Second Border
350-26

In a stunning array of "Yours Truly" fabrics, Eleanor's stars shine boldly against a soft, beige background. She framed her setting with rich deep rose, bordered with Caramel Rose Remembrance giving her lap robe a romantic look.

64" x 80"

Pieced by Eleanor Burns
Quilted by Carol Selepec

How to Select Your Fabric

Select a dark for the Stars, dark medium for the large Chain squares, and two light mediums for the two small squares made from Four-Patches. For interest, vary the scales of the prints. The Star center or large Chain square could be fussy cut. Select a tone on tone Background.

In this example, the dark Framing Border defines the pattern, and the large scale floral border pulls all the fabrics together.

Yardage

	Finished Block Size 16½" square on point	Wallhanging 3 x 3 = 9 total 65" x 65"	Lap 3 x 4 = 12 total 65" x 82"
Paste Your Fabric Here	**Background** Side Triangles Corner Triangles Star Points Squares Four-Patches	2½ yds (1) 18" strip cut into (2) 18" squares (2) 10" squares (2) 5" strips (8) 4½" strips cut into (64) 4½" squares (4) 2½" strips	3½ yds (2) 18" strips cut into (3) 18" squares (2) 10" squares (2) 5" strips (11) 4½" strips cut into (86) 4½" squares (6) 2½" strips
Paste Your Fabric Here	**Darkest** Star Centers Star Points	⅝ yd (1) 4½" strip cut into (4) 4½" squares (2) 6" strips	⅝ yd (1) 4½" strip cut into (6) 4½" squares (2) 6" strips
Paste Your Fabric Here	**Dark** Chain	¼ yd (1) 4½" strip cut into (9) 4½" squares	⅓ yd (2) 4½" strips cut into (12) 4½" squares
Paste Your Fabric Here	**First Medium** Four-Patches	¼ yd (2) 2½" strips	⅓ yd (3) 2½" strips
Paste Your Fabric Here	**Second Medium** Four-Patches	¼ yd (2) 2½" strips	⅓ yd (3) 2½" strips
Paste Your Fabric Here	**First Border**	½ yd (6) 2½" strips	⅝ yd (7) 2½" strips
Paste Your Fabric Here	**Second Border**	1⅛ yds (6) 6" strips	1⅓ yds (7) 6" strips
Paste Your Fabric Here	**Binding**	¾ yd (7) 3" strips	¾ yd (8) 3" strips
Paste Your Fabric Here	**Backing**	4 yds	5 yds
	Batting	72" x 72"	72" x 90"

Twin 3 x 5 = 15 total 68" x 101"	Full/Queen 5 x 5 = 25 total 101" x 101"	King 6 x 6 = 36 total 117" x 117"

4¼ yds
    (2) 18" strips cut into
        (3) 18" squares
    (2) 10" squares
    (3) 5" strips
    (14) 4½" strips cut into
        (108) 4½" squares
    (6) 2½" strips
	6 yds
	    (2) 18" strips cut into
	        (4) 18" squares
	    (2) 10" squares
	    (6) 5" strips
	    (23) 4½" strips cut into
	        (184) 4½" squares
	    (10) 2½" strips
		8¾ yds
		    (3) 18" strips cut into
		        (5) 18" squares
		    (2) 10" squares
		    (9) 5" strips
		    (34) 4½" strips cut into
		        (268) 4½" squares
		    (16) 2½" strips

¾ yd
    (1) 4½" strip cut into
        (8) 4½" squares
    (3) 6" strips
	1⅓ yds
	    (2) 4½" strips cut into
	        (16) 4½" squares
	    (6) 6" strips
		2⅛ yds
		    (4) 4½" strips cut into
		        (25) 4½" squares
		    (9) 6" strips

⅓ yd
    (2) 4½" strips cut into
        (15) 4½" squares
	½ yd
	    (3) 4½" strips cut into
	        (25) 4½" squares
		⅝ yd
		    (4) 4½" strips cut into
		        (36) 4½" squares

⅓ yd
    (3) 2½" strips
	½ yd
	    (5) 2½" strips
		⅔ yd
		    (8) 2½" strips

⅓ yd
    (3) 2½" strips
	½ yd
	    (5) 2½" strips
		⅔ yd
		    (8) 2½" strips

¾ yd
    (7) 3" strips
	⅞ yd
	    (9) 3" strips
		1 yd
		    (10) 3" strips

2 yds
    (9) 7" strips
	2⅛ yds
	    (10) 7" strips
		2¼ yds
		    (11) 7" strips

⅞ yd
    (9) 3" strips
	1 yd
	    (10) 3" strips
		1 yd
		    (11) 3" strips

6 yds	9 yds	10½ yds
76" x 108"	108" x 108"	125" x 125"

Making Stars

This pattern uses Triangle in a Square rulers from Quilt in a Day. If you do not own these rulers, make your own templates from patterns on pages 114-115.

1. Keep 6" Star Point strip folded **wrong sides together. This step is essential for mirror image pieces.** Place selvage edges on left, and trim.

2. With 6" Square Up ruler, layer cut **two pairs** of 3" x 6" rectangles per Star.

3" x 6" Pairs of Rectangles	
Wallhanging	8
Lap	12
Twin	16
Full/Queen	32
King	50

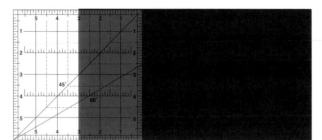

Cut two pairs 3" x 6" rectangles per Star.

3. **Layer cut** on one diagonal.

4. Sort these Star Point triangles so they are right sides up.

5. **Triangle ruler:** Place 5" Background strip right side up. Place Triangle ruler on strip, **accurately lining up narrow part** of triangle with top of strip. The bottom is not as critical.

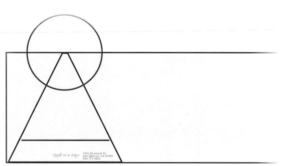

You should get twelve triangles per strip.

6. Cut four Background triangles per Star with rotary cutter, turning ruler with each cut.

Number of Triangles	
Wallhanging	16
Lap	24
Twin	32
Full/Queen	64
King	100

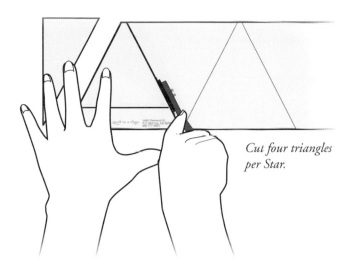

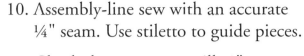

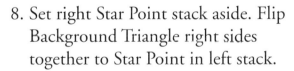

Cut four triangles per Star.

10. Assembly-line sew with an accurate ¼" seam. Use stiletto to guide pieces.

11. Check that seams are still ¼" at points.

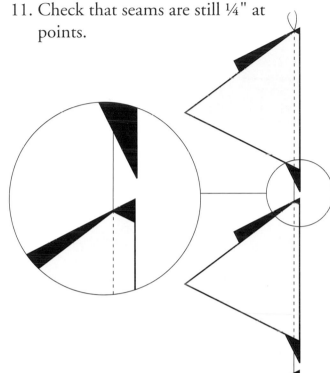

7. Lay out Background Triangles with base at bottom. Place Star Points on both sides. Make sure all fabrics are turned right side up.

Make four identical pieces per Star.

8. Set right Star Point stack aside. Flip Background Triangle right sides together to Star Point in left stack.

9. Position triangles so Star extends beyond Background at top, creating a tip at flat top. Star also extends at bottom.

12. Place on pressing mat with Star on top. Set seams, open, and press toward Star.

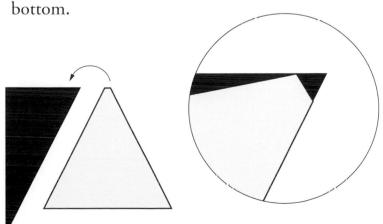

105

13. Place remaining Star Point stack to right of Background.

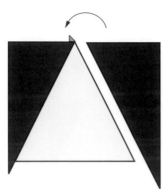

14. Flip right sides together, lining top tip of both pieces together.

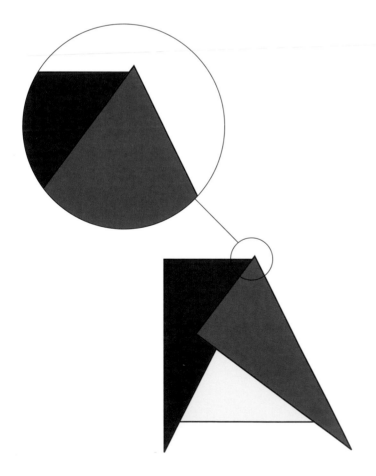

15. Assembly-line sew.

16. Set seams with Star on top, open, and press toward Star.

Make four identical pieces per Star.

Squaring Up Triangle in a Square Patches

Patches are squared to 4½" with seam ¼" from top, and ⅛" from corners.

1. Place patch on small cutting mat or a "lazy Susan" turntable mat.

2. **Triangle in a Square Ruler:**
   Place 4½" square ruler on patch. Line up green triangle lines on ruler with seams.

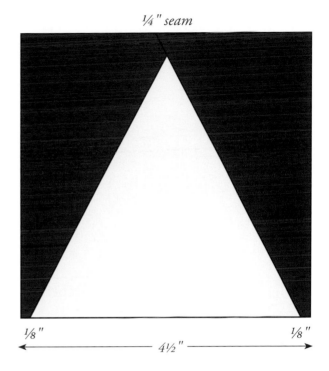

¼" seam

⅛"   4½"   ⅛"

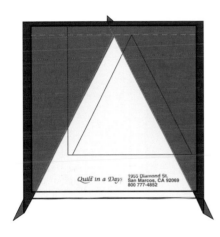

3. Trim patch on right side and top.

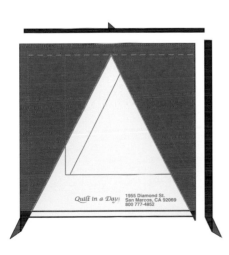

4. Turn mat. Trim patch on remaining two sides to 4½" square.

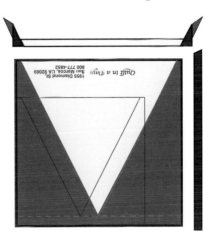

Sewing Star Blocks Together

1. Count out Star Points and 4½" Star Center squares with 4½" Background squares. Stack pieces equal to number of Stars.

Number of Stars	
Wallhanging	4
Lap	6
Twin	8
Full/Queen	16
King	25

2. Flip middle vertical row to patches on left.

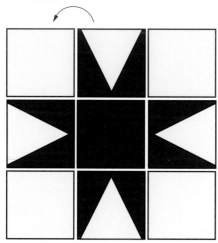

3. Matching outside edges, assembly-line sew.

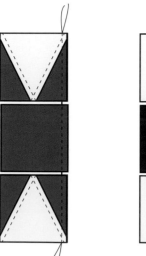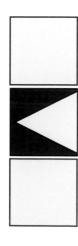

4. Flip right vertical row to middle row.

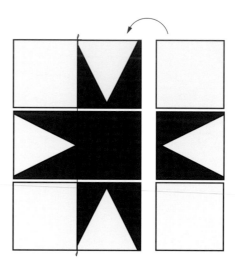

5. Assembly-line sew.

6. Clip apart after each Star, or every third row.

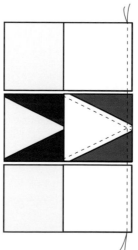

7. Flip row on right to middle row. Press seams away from Star Points, and lock together.

8. Assembly-line sew. Clip Stars apart.

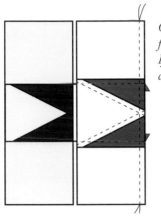

Check points from right side. If necessary, change seam.

9. Flip middle row to last row, press seams away from Star Points, lock, and assembly-line sew.

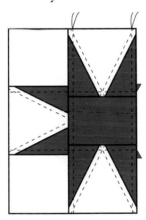

10. Clip Stars apart, and press final seams away from center row.

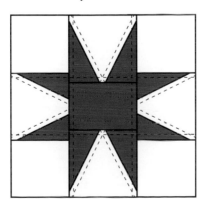

Making Four-Patches

1. Cut Background and Four-Patch strips in half and turn right side up. Divide Background strips into two equal stacks. Line up cut edges at top.

2. Sew 2½" Background and Four-Patch strips right sides together. Use an accurate ¼" seam.

3. Set seams with Four-Patch strip on top, open, and press against seam.

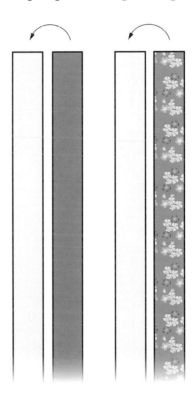

4. Measure width of strips. They should measure 4½".

5. Layer first Four-Patch strip right side up on gridded cutting mat with Background across top. Place second Four-Patch strip right sides together to it with Four-Patch across top. Lock seams. Line up strips with grid.

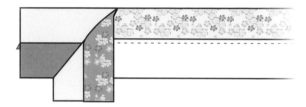

6. Square left end. Cut 2½" pairs from each strip set. Stack on spare ruler to carry to sewing area.

Number of 2½" Pairs	
Wallhanging	24
Lap	34
Twin	44
Full/Queen	80
King	120

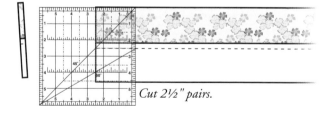

Cut 2½" pairs.

7. Matching outside edges and center seam, assembly-line sew. Use stiletto to hold outside edges together and seams flat.

8. Remove three stitches on each side of center.

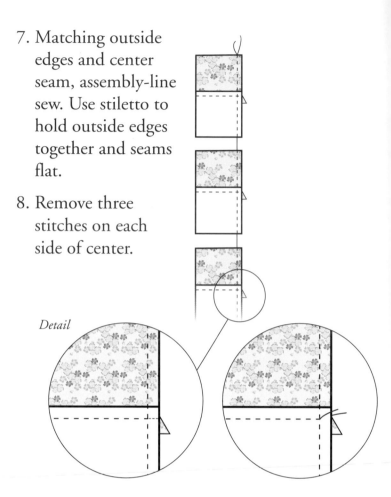

Detail

9. Open and place wrong side up on pressing mat. Flatten center seam, creating a small Four-Patch. Press seams.

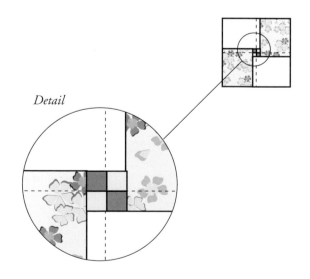

Detail

110

Making Center Chain Blocks

1. Stack Four-Patches with 4½" Background squares and 4½" Center squares.

Number in each stack	
Wallhanging	1
Lap	2
Twin	3
Full/Queen	9
King	16

2. Flip middle vertical row to patches on left.

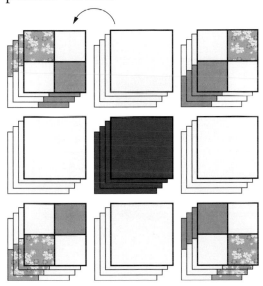

3. Matching outside edges, assembly-line sew.

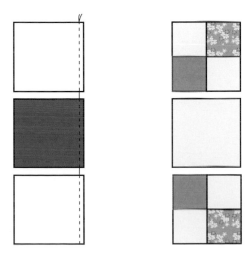

4. Flip right vertical row to middle row. Assembly-line sew.

5. Clip apart after each Center Chain block, or every third row.

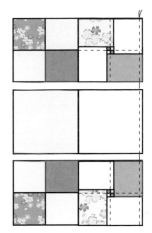

6. Flip row on right to middle row. Press seams away from Center Square and Four-Patches. Lock seams together.

7. Assembly-line sew.

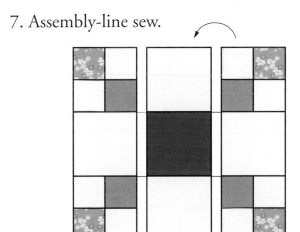

8. Flip last row to block, press seams away from Center and Four-Patches, lock, and assembly-line sew.

9. Clip Chain block apart, and press final seams toward center row.

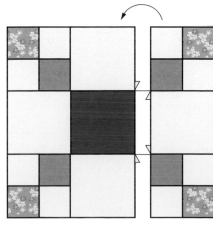

Making Side Chain Blocks

1. Stack Four-Patches with 4½"
   Background squares and 4½" Chain
   squares.

Number in each Stack	
Wallhanging	4
Lap	6
Twin	8
Full/Queen	12
King	16

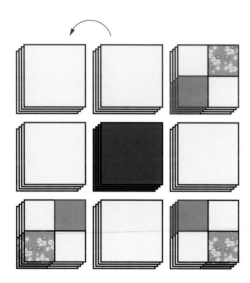

2. Assembly-line sew. Press seams away
   from Chain square and Four-Patches,
   locking seams together.

3. Clip Side Chain blocks apart, and
   press final seams toward center row.

Making Corner Chain Blocks

1. Stack Four-Patches with 4½"
   Background squares and 4½" Chain
   squares.

Number in each Stack	
Wallhanging	4
Lap	4
Twin	4
Full/Queen	4
King	4

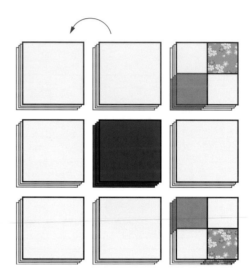

2. Assembly-line sew. Press seams away
   from Chain and Four-Patches, locking
   seams together.

3. Clip Corner Chain blocks apart, and
   press final seams toward center row.

Sewing Top Together

1. **Side Triangles:** Cut 18" Background Squares on both diagonals into four triangles.

Number of 18" Squares	
Wallhanging	2
Lap	3
Twin	3
Full/Queen	4
King	5

2. **Corner Triangles:** Cut two 10" Background Squares on one diagonal into two triangles each.

Number of 10" Squares	
Wallhanging	2
Lap	2
Twin	2
Full/Queen	2
King	2

3. Lay out blocks in diagonal rows.

4. Sew diagonal rows together, locking seams on Star blocks with Chain blocks.

5. Trim tips on Side Triangles even with rows.

6. Press seams away from Chain blocks.

7. Sew rows together.

8. Sew Corners to quilt top last. Press seams toward Corners.

9. Turn to **Finishing Instructions**, page 226.

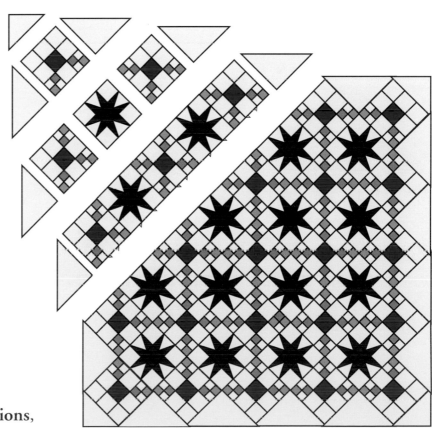

Triangle in a Square Templates

The Triangle in a Square rulers are available on heavy plexiglas from Quilt in a Day. Cutting with these rulers makes the process easier, and cut pieces are more accurate.

If you do not have these rulers, tape template plastic to these pages, trace templates with colored sharp markers, and cut out on the outside lines.

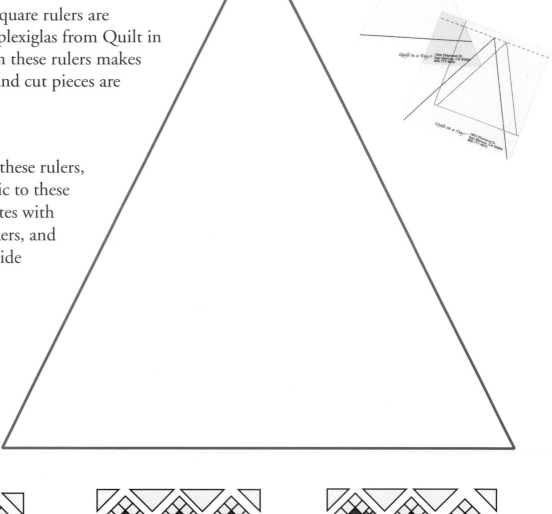

Wallhanging

Lap Robe

Twin

When indicated to use Triangle in a Square rulers, trace around the triangle template with a marking pen, and rotary cut on the lines with a 6" x 12" ruler.

Tape the square template to the underneath side in upper right corner of a plexiglas 6" x 6" ruler and use as instructed.

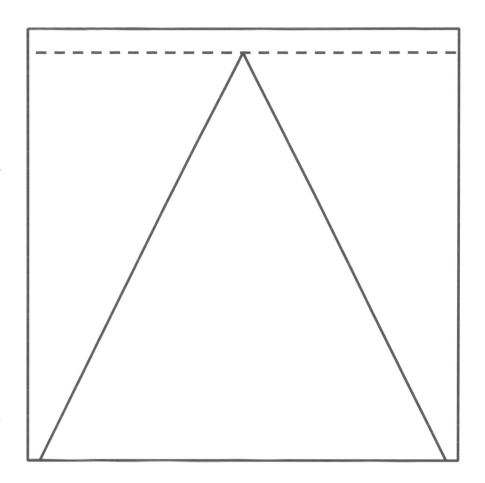

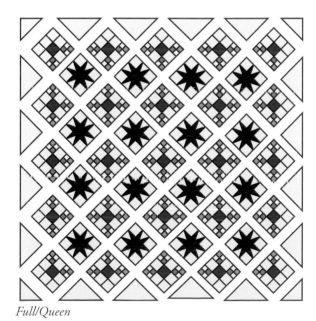

Full/Queen

King

Stars and Four-Patches Quilt

My staff is a galaxy of radiant stars in my life, always coming forth with stellar performances. My students are glorious bits of color sewn into charming four-patches, delighting me with their brilliant accomplishments. It's fitting that staff and students become one constellation as Stars and Four-Patches.

We love to entertain each other at Camp Cedar Glen in Julian during our semi-annual retreat. At this particular event, my "four-patches" put on an impromptu fashion show. I started out garbed in a cotton dress with plunging neckline, balloon hemline, and pillbox hat. My students quickly came up with entries including a bare midriff, box collar, jumper with rolled collar, and a smoking jacket with wing tip shoes, among other hilarious bits of costuming.

When the book *Stars Across America* was published in 1996, Quilt in a Day teachers pieced together outfits to represent the heroic women featured. Luann Stout rallied for the vote as Susan B. Anthony. Janice Orr toted a copy of Uncle Tom's Cabin as Harriet Beecher Stowe. Anne Cann was sweeping liquor out of town as Frances Willard. Anne Dease as Sojourner Truth declared "Ain't I a woman!" Dixie Mulligan sported tools of the trade as Clara Barton, and Sue Bouchard shouted "Shoot this old gray head" as Barbara Frietchie. Leading everyone was Sheila Meehan as Harriet Tubman.

Quilt in a Day employees gathered for an annual holiday photo. Company mascot Peanut Burns made sure she was included in the festivities.

Fabric Selection

For a scrappy look, Julia selected reproduction 30's fabric in an array of colors. Her stars appear to radiate by her creative use of the star center fabrics echoed for her chains. She created a Seminole border with her scraps to perfectly frame her lap robe.

Pieced by Julia Markovitz
Quilted by Nancy Letchworth
62" x 76"

In honor of her grandmother, Sue cleverly fussy cut owls for her star centers and made her points from coordinating fabrics. The chain, a "read as solid" black print, is striking against an ivory background. The simple owl print border frames the quilt for a bold and masculine effect.

Pieced and Quilted by Sue Bouchard
52" x 80"

For her lap robe, Nancy took a holiday approach with dark and medium reds and greens set against a small scale print of red and green on a white background. Her Seminole border in dark green really sets her quilt off. Seasons Greetings!

Pieced and Quilted
by Nancy Letchworth
62" x 76"

Yours Truly
Fabrics by
BENARTEX
INCORPORATED

In perfect harmony, soft green chains set on a creamy background grace Sue's deep purple and sage stars. She extends the deep purple in her Seminole border to compliment her color scheme and completes her quilt with the lilac Floral Garden fabric.

Pieced by Sue Bouchard
Quilted by Sandy Thompson
62" x 76"

Dark #1
Star Points

Seminole 2

350-66

Medium #1
Star Center

Seminole 3

Outside Borders

352-60

Dark #2
Star Points

Binding

350-44

Medium #2
Star Center

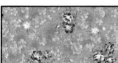

352-49

Background

Framing Border

Seminole 1

241-07

Medium #3
Four-Patches

Cornerstones

355-40

How to Select Your Fabric

For each of the two Stars, select dark for points and medium for centers. Select an additional medium for Four-Patches and Cornerstones. The Four-Patches should not be darker than the Stars. Select a tone on tone Background. Repeat the dark and medium fabrics used in one of the Stars for the Seminole Border.

Stars are made with the Triangle in a Square rulers from Quilt in a Day. If you do not have the Triangle in a Square rulers, the templates are on pages 114 and 115.

Yardage

Finished Block Size 12" square	Wallhanging 2 x 2 = 4 total 49" x 49"	Lap 3 x 4 = 12 total 62" x 76"
Paste Your Fabric Here **Background** Triangles Four-Patches Lattice	1 yd (2) 5" strips (2) 2½" strips (4) 2½" strips	2¼ yds (4) 5" strips (6) 2½" strips (11) 2½" strips
Paste Your Fabric Here **Dark #1** Star Points	¼ yd (1) 6" strip	½ yd (2) 6" strips
Paste Your Fabric Here **Medium #1** Star Center	¼ yd (2) 4½" squares	¼ yd (1) 4½" strip cut into (6) 4½" squares
Paste Your Fabric Here **Dark #2** Star Points	½ yd (1) 6" strip	½ yd (2) 6" strips
Paste Your Fabric Here **Medium #2** Star Center	¼ yd (2) 4½" squares	¼ yd (1) 4½" strip cut into (6) 4½" squares
Paste Your Fabric Here **Medium #3** Four-Patches Cornerstones	¼ yd of each (2) 2½" strips (1) 2½" strip cut into (9) 2½" squares	¾ yd (6) 2½" strips (2) 2½" strips cut into (20) 2½" squares
Paste Your Fabric Here **Seminole Border** Background Framing Border Seminole	⅞ yd (4) 3" strips (3) 2¾" strips	1¼ yds (6) 3½" strips (5) 2¾" strips
Paste Your Fabric Here **Dark #1** Seminole Seminole Corners	⅜ yd (3) 2½" strips (4) 2½" squares	½ yd (5) 2½" strips (4) 2½" squares
Paste Your Fabric Here **Medium #1** Seminole Seminole Corners Seminole Corners Outside Border	1⅛ yds (3) 2¾" strips (4) 2½" x 2¾" (4) 2¾" squares (5) 4½" strips	1½ yds (5) 2¾" strips (4) 2½" x 2¾" (4) 2¾" squares (7) 4½" strips
Paste Your Fabric Here **Binding**	¾ yd (6) 3" strips	¾ yd (8) 3" strips
Backing	3¼ yds	4¾ yds
Batting	56" x 56"	70" x 84"

Twin	Full/Queen	King
3 x 5 = 15 total 65" x 93"	5 x 6 = 30 total 93" x 107"	6 x 6 = 36 total 107" x 107"
2½ yds (5) 5" strips (8) 2½" strips (13) 2½" strips	4¼ yds (9) 5" strips (15) 2½" strips (24) 2½" strips	5 yds (11) 5" strips (18) 2½" strips (28) 2½" strips
⅝ yd (3) 6" strips	1 yd (5) 6" strips	1¼ yds (6) 6" strips
¼ yd (1) 4½" strip cut into (8) 4½" squares	⅓ yd (2) 4½" strips cut into (15) 4½" squares	½ yd (3) 4½" strips cut into (18) 4½" squares
⅝ yd (3) 6" strips	1 yd (5) 6" strips	1¼ yds (6) 6" strips
¼ yd (1) 4½" strip cut into (7) 4½" squares	⅓ yd (2) 4½" strips cut into (15) 4½" squares	½ yd (3) 4½" strips cut into (18) 4½" squares
1 yd (8) 2½" strips (2) 2½" strips cut into (24) 2½" squares	1½ yds (15) 2½" strips (3) 2½" strips cut into (42) 2½" squares	1¾ yds (18) 2½" strips (4) 2½" strips cut into (49) 2½" squares
1½ yds (7) 3½" strips (6) 2¾" strips	1¾ yds (9) 3½" strips (8) 2¾" strips	2 yds (10) 3½" strips (9) 2¾" strips
⅔ yd (6) 2½" strips (4) 2½" squares	¾ yd (8) 2½" strips (4) 2½" squares	⅞ yd (9) 2½" strips (4) 2½" squares
2 yds (6) 2¾" strips (4) 2½" x 2¾" (4) 2¾" squares (9) 6½" strips	3 yds (8) 2¾" strips (4) 2½" x 2¾" (4) 2¾" squares (11) 6½" strips	3¼ yds (9) 2¾" strips (4) 2½" x 2¾" (4) 2¾" squares (12) 6½" strips
⅞ yd (9) 3" strips	1 yd (11) 3" strips	1¼ yds (12) 3" strips
6½ yds	9½ yds	10 yds
74" x 102"	102" x 118"	118" x 118"

Making Stars

This patterns uses Triangle in a Square rulers from Quilt in a Day. If you do not own these rulers, make your own templates from patterns on pages 114 – 115.

Repeat these steps from both Star fabrics.

1. Keep 6" Star Point strip folded **wrong sides together. This step is essential for mirror image pieces.** Place selvage edges on left, and trim.

2. With 6" Square Up ruler, layer cut **two pairs** of 3" x 6" rectangles per Star.

Cut two pairs 3" x 6" rectangles per Star.

Pairs of Rectangles	
Wallhanging	4
Lap	12
Twin	16
Full/Queen	30
King	36

Repeat from second fabric

3. **Layer cut on one diagonal.**

4. Sort Star Point triangles so they are right sides up.

5. **Triangle ruler:** Place 5" Background strip right side up. Place Triangle ruler on strip, **accurately lining up narrow part** of triangle with top of strip. The bottom is not as critical.

6. Cut four triangles per Star with rotary cutter, turning ruler with each cut.

Number of Triangles	
Wallhanging	16
Lap	48
Twin	60
Full/Queen	120
King	144

You should get twelve triangles per strip.

7. Make Star Points from two sets of fabrics following directions on pages 104 – 107.

	Star 1	Star 2
Wallhanging	8	8
Lap	24	24
Twin	32	28
Full/Queen	60	60
King	72	72

8. Square patches to 4½".

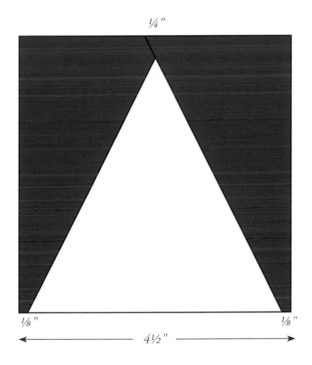

Making Four-Patches

Sew test set of strips. Width should measure 4½".

1. Cut 2½" Background and Four-Patch strips in half.

2. Sew half strips right sides together. Use an accurate ¼" seam.

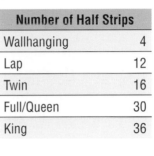

Number of Half Strips	
Wallhanging	4
Lap	12
Twin	16
Full/Queen	30
King	36

3. Set seams with Four-Patch strip on top, open, and press toward Four-Patch.

4. Measure width of strips. They should measure 4½". Adjust seam if necessary.

5. Layer first strip right side up on gridded cutting mat with Background across top. Place second strip right sides together to it with Four-Patch across top. Lock seams. Line up strips with grid.

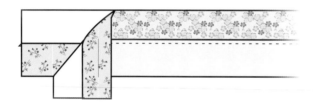

6. Square left end. Cut 2½" pairs from each strip set. Stack on spare ruler to carry to sewing area.

Number of Four-Patches	
Wallhanging	16
Lap	48
Twin	60
Full/Queen	120
King	144

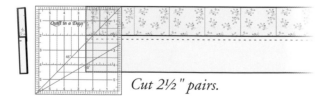

Cut 2½" pairs.

7. Matching outside edges and center seam, assembly-line sew. Use stiletto to hold outside edges together and seams flat.

8. Repeat with all pieces for Four-Patches.

9. Remove the three stitches on each side of center indicated in red thread.

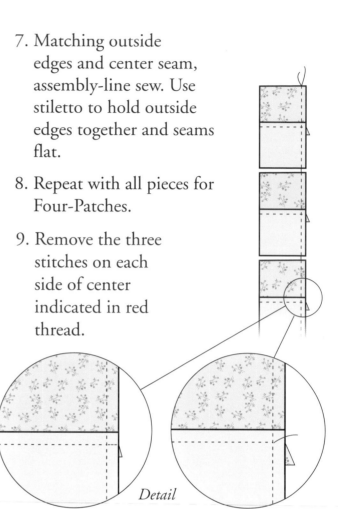

Detail

10. Open and place wrong side up on pressing mat. Flatten center seam, creating a small Four-Patch. Press seams.

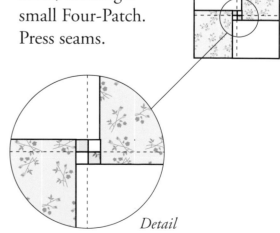

Detail

Sewing Star Blocks Together

1. Count out Star Points and 4½" Star Center squares with 4½" Four-Patches. Stack pieces per Star.

Number in each stack		
Wallhanging	2	2
Lap	6	6
Twin	8	7
Full/Queen	15	15
King	18	18

2. Flip middle vertical row to patches on left.

3. Matching outside edges, assembly-line sew.

4. Flip right vertical row to middle row.

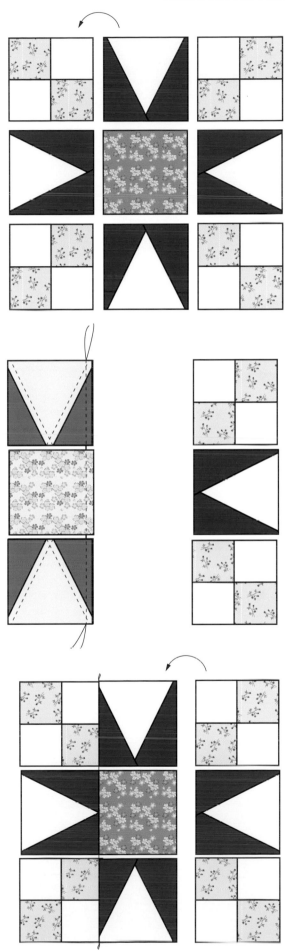

5. Assembly-line sew.

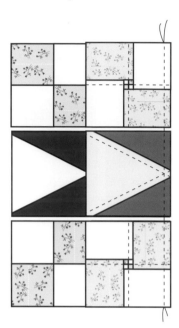

6. Clip apart after each Star, or every third row.

7. Turn block one quarter turn. Flip row on right to middle row. Press seams away from Star Points, and lock together.

8. Assembly-line sew.

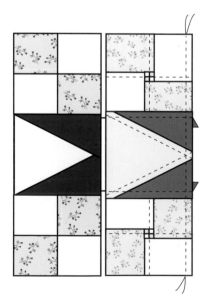

9. Sew last row, pressing seams away from Star Points.

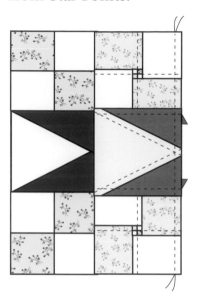

10. Clip Stars apart, and press final seams away from center row.

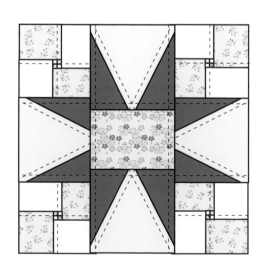

Laying Out Quilt Top

1. Measure pressed Star. Star should be approximately 12½"square.

2. Cut 2½" Lattice strips same length as Star. Cut 2½" square Cornerstones.

	Lattice	Cornerstones
Wallhanging	12	9
Lap	31	20
Twin	38	24
Full/Queen	71	42
King	84	49

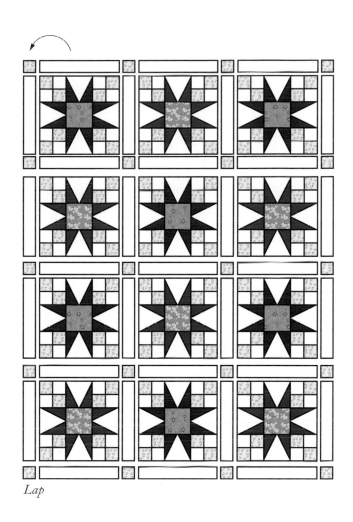

Lap

3. Place two sets of Stars in alternating order.

4. Place 2½" Lattice strips and 2½" Cornerstones between Star blocks.

5. Assembly-line sew all vertical rows.

6. Assembly-line sew remaining rows, pressing seams toward Lattice.

Layouts

Wallhanging

Lap

Full/Queen

Twin

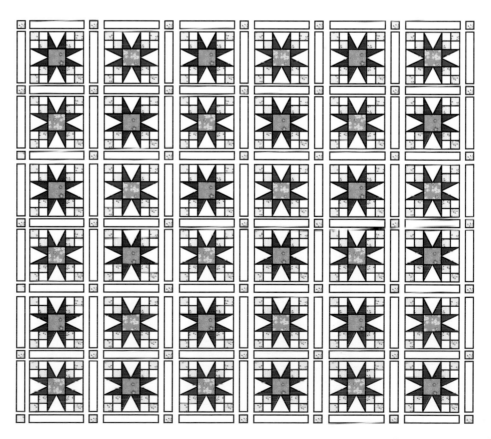

King

Sewing Framing Border to Top

1. Sew Background strips to four sides. Press seams toward Border.

2. Mark a dot ¼" from outside edge on four corners. Place pin in center of each side.

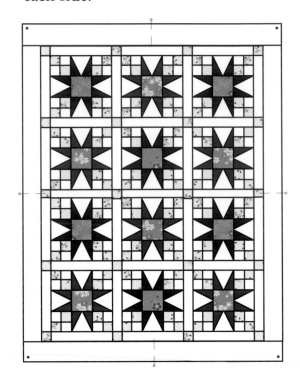

2. Set seams with dark fabric on top, open, and press toward dark.

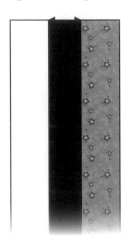

3. Layer several sets of strips on cutting mat. Square left ends.

4. Layer cut 2½" pieces.

Number of Pieces	
Wallhanging	48
Lap	78
Twin	90
Full/Queen	120
King	128

Making Seminole Borders

1. Stack strips in this order and assembly-line sew.

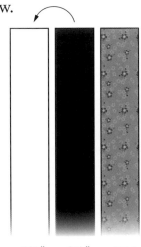

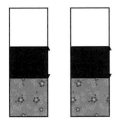

2¾"   2½"   2¾"
Background   *Dark #1*   *Medium #1*

5. Count out pieces for four sides.

	Two Sides	Top and Bottom
Wallhanging	12	12
Lap	22	17
Twin	28	17
Full/Queen	32	28
King	32	32

6. Sew one side together at a time. Divide one side into two stacks. Place so that right stack is one step lower than left stack.

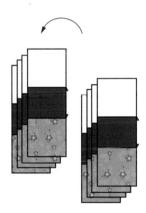

7. Flip piece on right to piece on left.

8. Match and fingerpin seams.

9. Assembly-line sew all pieces. Clip connecting threads.

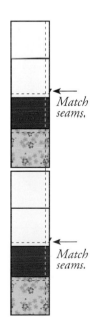

Match seams.

Match seams.

10. Continue to assembly-line sew until all pieces from one side are sewn together. Make certain each new piece is one step lower than previous one.

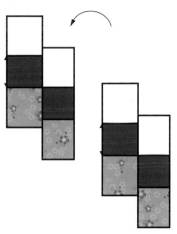

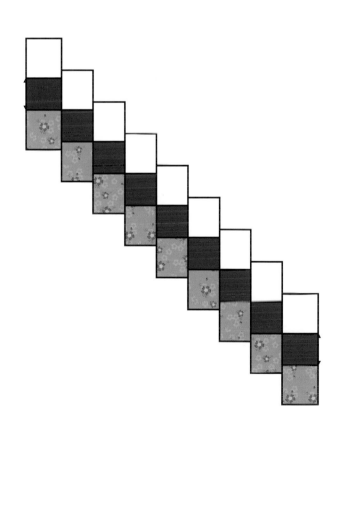

Making Four Corners

1. Sew four 2½" dark squares to four 2½" x 2¾" medium rectangles.

2. Press seams toward dark square.

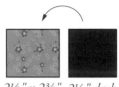
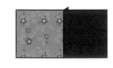

2½" x 2¾" medium   *2½" dark*

3. Sew to a 2¾" medium square.

4. Press seam toward 2¾" medium square.

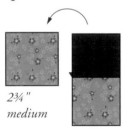

2¾" medium

5. Place Seminole strips right side up with Background across bottom. Sew corners to right ends of Seminole. Match seam. Background is ¼" longer.

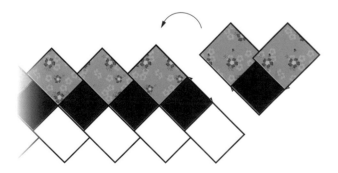

6. Place Seminole strips wrong sides up with Background on top. Press seams toward left.

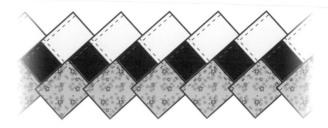

7. Press on right side.

Trimming Seminole

1. From right side, line up ¼" line on 6" x 24" ruler with dark points, and with peak on outside corner. Trim off tips on Background side of Seminole.

2. Outside Corners are trimmed to peaks because there is no seam.

3. On wrong side, mark a dot ¼" in from outside edge on both sides for miter. Place pin in center of each side.

Sewing Seminole to Sides

1. Measure Seminole against sides of quilt top.

2. If Seminole is longer, take a deeper seam on several segments. If Seminole is shorter, trim Framing Border strips.

3. Pin Seminole right sides together to sides of quilt, matching ¼" marks and center pins.

4. Beginning at ¼" dot, sew through all thicknesses with Seminole on bottom. Ease if necessary.

5. Flip out, and finger press seam toward Framing Border.

Sewing Seminole to Top and Bottom

1. Pin top and bottom Seminole right sides together to quilt, matching ¼" marks and center pins.

2. Beginning at ¼" dot, sew through all thicknesses with Seminole on bottom.

3. Flip out, and finger press seam toward Framing Border.

4. Match and pin corners for miter.

5. Backstitch to ¼" mark, leave ¼" open, and sew to outer edge.

6. Press mitered seam corner open.

7. Trim outside Seminole corners with 12½" Square Up ruler, and sides with 6" x 24" ruler.

8. Add Outside Border.

9. Turn to **Finishing Instructions** on page 226.

Gadabout Quilt

What fun I've had, from teaching 600 students to go "Agog" in a tent in Paducah, Kentucky, to 50 students appliquing on a Mississippi riverboat, and 25 students "giving it a spin" at Moore's Sewing in Huntington Beach, California.

Teaching is my favorite thing to do - and students make each class unique and enjoyable.

Now I know why I'm weary! In the first four months of my anniversary year, I have spent 27,000 miles gadding about the country. That equates to 45 days on the road - or 45 strange beds!

Fabric Selection

Nancy created a carnival mood with her use of reds and blues harmonized with tan. She designed hourglass blocks on a smaller scale to complete her festive look in this stunning lap robe.

Pieced by Nancy Loftis
Quilted by Debra Jenks
45" x 55"

Reproduction 30's fabric gives an old fashioned look to Eleanor's crib quilt. Dark pink pinwheels stand out to delight any baby.

Pieced by Eleanor Burns
Quilted by Carol Selepec
42" x 52"

Shades of sage green and cream compliment each other to lend a tone of sophistication to Patricia's wallhanging. Dark navy hourglasses stand out, while medium pinwheels recede. To frame her design, she fussy cut a border stripe for a flattering finish.

Pieced by Patricia Knoechel
Quilted by Teresa Varnes
42" x 42"

Marie selected Yours Truly fabrics for her quilt in lilac, purple and sage tones. She blended them to create a kaleidoscopic look and framed it with deep purple to set off her design.

Light
Hourglass

356-30

Dark Hourglass

Dark
First Border

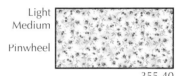

350-66

Light
Medium

Pinwheel

355-40

Dark
Medium

Pinwheel

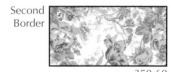

352-60

Second
Border

350-60

Pieced by Marie Harper
Quilted by Carol Selepec

64" x 94"

How to Select Your Fabric

Select one light and one dark fabric for the part of the block that looks like an hourglass, and one light medium and one dark medium for the pinwheel.

In the sample quilt, a large scale deep purple that reads solid from a distance pairs with a light fabric fresh with a small scale bouquet of flowers. The deep purple hourglass stands out, and the medium pinwheel recedes into the quilt. Reverse values if you prefer the pinwheel to stand out. The pinwheels are light medium small scale roses and dark medium purple flowers. The same dark frames the blocks, with an additional large scale floral border on a linen textured background.

Yardage

	Finished Block Size 10" square	Wallhanging 3 x 3 = 9 total 39" x 39"	Lap 3 x 4 = 12 total 42" x 52"
Paste Your Fabric Here	**Light** Hourglass	½ yd (5) 2½" strips	½ yd (6) 2½" strips
Paste Your Fabric Here	**Dark** Hourglass	½ yd (5) 2½" strips	½ yd (6) 2½" strips
Paste Your Fabric Here	**Light Medium** Pinwheel	½ yd (2) 6½" strips cut into (9) 6½" squares	½ yd (2) 6½" strips cut into (12) 6½" squares
Paste Your Fabric Here	**Dark Medium** Pinwheel	½ yd (2) 6½" strips cut into (9) 6½" squares	½ yd (2) 6½" strips cut into (12) 6½" squares
Paste Your Fabric Here	**First Border**	⅜ yd (4) 2" strips	½ yd (5) 2½" strips
Paste Your Fabric Here	**Second Border**	½ yd (4) 4" strips	1 yd (6) 5½" strips
Paste Your Fabric Here	**Binding**	½ yd (5) 3" strips	⅝ yd (6) 3" strips
	Backing	1¼ yds	2¾ yds
	Batting	45" x 45"	50" x 60"

Pieced and Quilted by
Nancy Letchworth
42" x 52"

Twin	Full/Queen	King
5 x 8 = 40 total 68" x 98"	8 x 8 = 64 total 96" x 96"	9 x 9 = 81 total 106" x 106"

1½ yds
  (20) 2½" strips
	2½ yds
	  (32) 2½" strips
		3 yds
		  (41) 2½" strips

1½ yds
  (20) 2½" strips
	2½ yds
	  (32) 2½" strips
		3 yds
		  (41) 2½" strips

1½ yds
  (7) 6½" strips cut into
    (40) 6½" squares
	2⅛ yds
	  (11) 6½" strips cut into
	    (64) 6½" squares
		2¾ yds
		  (14) 6½" strips cut into
		    (81) 6½" squares

1½ yds
  (7) 6½" strips cut into
    (40) 6½" squares
	2⅛ yds
	  (11) 6½" strips cut into
	    (64) 6½" squares
		2¾ yds
		  (14) 6½" strips cut into
		    (81) 6½" squares

¾ yd
  (7) 3½" strips
	1 yd
	  (8) 3½" strips
		1⅛ yds
		  (10) 3½" strips

2 yds
  (9) 7½" strips
	2¼ yds
	  (10) 7½" strips
		2½ yds
		  (11) 7½" strips

⅞ yd
  (9) 3" strips
	1 yd
	  (10) 3" strips
		1⅛ yds
		  (12) 3" strips

6 yds	9 yds	10 yds
78" x 108"	108" x 108"	118" x 118"

Making Hourglass

Use an accurate ¼ " seam and 15 stitches per inch, or 2.0.

1. Sew 2½" Light and 2½" Dark selvage to selvage strips right sides together.

2½" Strips	
Wallhanging	5
Lap	6
Twin	20
Full/Queen	32
King	41

2. Set seams with Dark on top.

3. Open, and press toward Dark.

4. Place one strip along line on cutting mat, with Dark across top.

5. Turn 6½" Triangle Square Up ruler on point. Line up top point of ruler with top edge of strip. Line up diagonal line on ruler with bottom of strip, approximately 6¼" to 6½". Cut triangle shape.

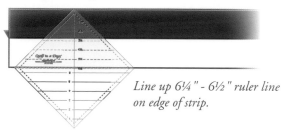

Line up 6¼ " - 6½ " ruler line on edge of strip.

6. Move ruler over, and cut second triangle shape.

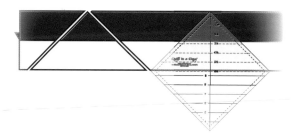

7. Continue cutting triangle shapes. Turn ruler around to cut last triangle. Pieces are oversized and will be squared later.

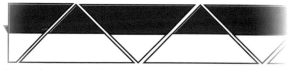

Cut eight triangles from each strip.

8. Make two stacks. From each strip, there should be four of one, and four of the other. Set aside.

Making Pinwheels

1. Use contrasting thread to see stitching.

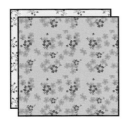

2. Place Light Medium and Dark Medium 6½" squares right sides together. **Always keep Dark Medium fabric on top.**

Number of Pairs	
Wallhanging	9
Lap	12
Twin	40
Full/Queen	64
King	81

3. Draw two diagonal lines.

4. Sew ¼" seam down left side of one diagonal line, stopping at center.

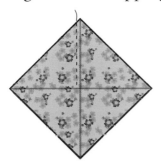

5. Leave needle in fabric, pivot, and sew on center line toward center. Stop ¼" past diagonal center line.

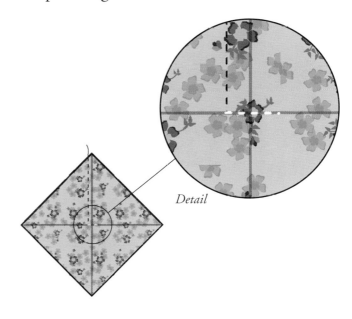

Detail

6. Pivot again and stitch ¼" from right side of diagonal line.

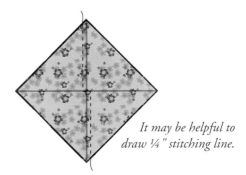

It may be helpful to draw ¼" stitching line.

7. Turn. Repeat on second diagonal line.

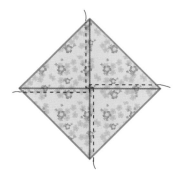

8. Cut apart on both drawn diagonal lines.

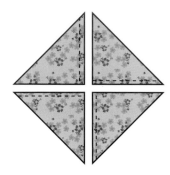

9. Set seams with Dark Medium on top.

10. Open, and press toward Dark Medium.

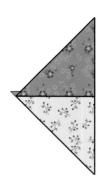

Finishing 5½" Patches

1. Lay out Pinwheel patches with Hourglass patches. Make two different sets.

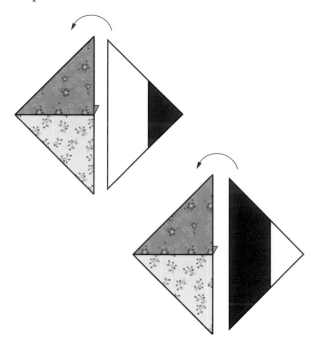

2. Flip right sides together, keeping points aligned. Assembly-line sew.

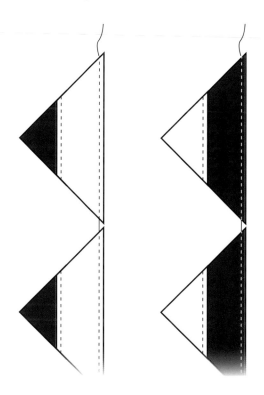

3. Cut apart, keeping two stacks separated.

Squaring Blocks to 5½"

1. Turn both stacks wrong side up with two Medium Triangles on top. Keep two separate stacks.

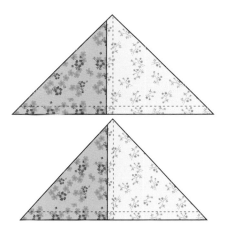

2. Use Triangle Square Up ruler to square patch to 5½". Place ruler's 5½" diagonal line on horizontal stitching line. Place ruler's vertical line on vertical stitches.

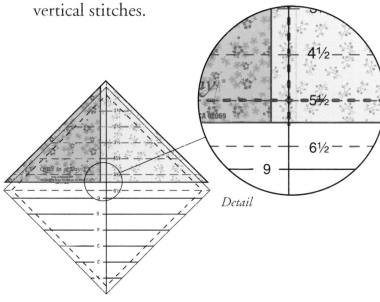

Detail

3. Trim two sides. Open and check first trimmed patch to see if it measures 5½" square.

4. Square all patches. Keep two separate stacks.

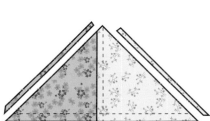

Pressing Blocks Open

Seams in one stack are pressed in one direction, and seams in remaining stack are pressed in other direction, so pieces lock together.

1. Select stack with long Dark piece. Place Dark piece on top.

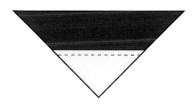

2. Set seams, open, and press seams toward Dark piece.

3. Trim tips with rotary cutter or scissors.

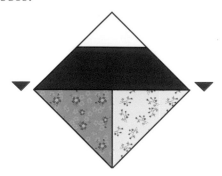

4. Place remaining stack with long Light piece underneath, and two Medium triangles on top.

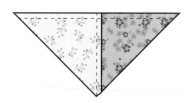

5. Set seams, open, and press seams toward Medium triangles. Trim tips.

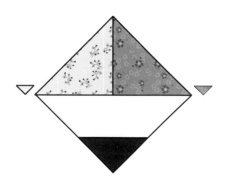

Sewing Block Together

1. Lay out four patches. Stack patches equal to number of blocks.

Blocks	
Wallhanging	9
Lap	12
Twin	40
Full/Queen	64
King	81

2. Flip patch on right to patch on left, right sides together. Lock seams.

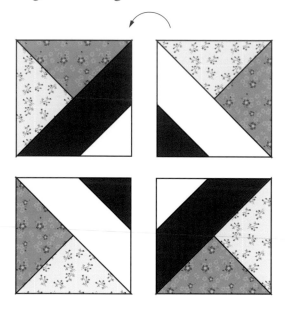

3. Assembly-line sew stacks. Clip apart between blocks.

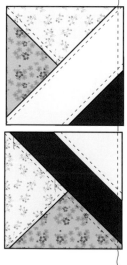

4. Open and flip patches right sides together.

5. Push top seam upward and underneath seam downward. Lock center seams. Assembly-line sew blocks.

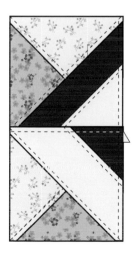

Push top seam upward and underneath seam downward.

6. At center seam, cut first stitch with scissors. See circle.

Detail

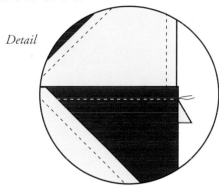

7. Unsew the three vertical stitches at the center with stiletto or seam ripper. Unsew stitches on other side.

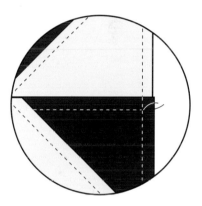

8. Open center seams and push down flat to form a tiny Four-Patch. Press new seams clockwise around center.

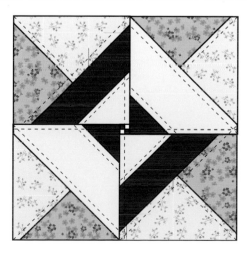

Laying Out Top

1. Lay out blocks, alternating direction of Dark strips.

Blocks	
Wallhanging	3 x 3
Lap	3 x 4
Twin	5 x 8
Full/Queen	8 x 8
King	9 x 9

2. Flip second vertical row to first vertical row. Stack with top block on top. Assembly-line sew vertical rows. See **Sewing Vertical Rows** on page 226.

3. Sew horizontal rows. Push seams between blocks in opposite directions.

4. Press on the wrong side. Press on the right side.

5. Add Borders.

6. Turn to **Finishing Instructions**, page 226.

Cornerstones of My Life

I have fortunately been surrounded by a patchwork of many lives. My mom taught me the joy of sewing, and I learned business at the dining table with my dad as head.

My sons, Orion and Grant, have always been pillars of strength. They are both successful, Orion as General Manager for Quilt in a Day, and Grant as owner of BBS Manufacturing, manufacturer and distributor of skateboards.

Assistants Teresa Varnes and Sue Bouchard are always behind the scenes, working very hard to make me look good. And you thought I did it all!

Pennsylvania cousin Carol Ann Selepec breathes life into my quilts with her award winning long arm quilting. We started years ago sewing juvenile dolls together.

Merritt Voigtlander has excelled at taking our art department from Commodore computers and waxed art boards to high technology and design.

Best friend Brian Steutel describes himself as "my secret weapon." I can count on him to turn my impossible dreams into reality.

Fabric Selection

With creamy chains criss-crossing her quilt, Laura chose her peach and green blocks to burst forth in this charming queen sized quilt. Her first border, in cream, provides just the right frame for this lovely quilt.

*Pieced and Quilted
by Laurie McCauley
98" x 98"*

Tone on tone deep green, pink, lavender and over-all floral fabric compliment each other in Sue's bold and beautiful quilt.

*Pieced by Sue Bouchard
Quilted by Sandy Thompson*

Print 1

Border

350-33

Print 2

352-48

Solid 3

354-01

Solid 4

354-49

Background

Framing
Border

241-07

With thoughts of spring in the air, Linda united Yours Truly pastels of pink, blue, green and yellow in her queen sized quilt. The yellow and pink fabric used in the quilt borders compliments the soft, flowery effect.

Pieced by Linda Parker
Quilted by Carol Selepec

95" x 95"

How to Select Your Fabric

Select two multi-colored prints for Print #1 and Print #2, and two small scale prints that read solid from a distance for Solid #3 and Solid #4. Label your fabrics accordingly.

In the sample quilt, Print #1 is beautiful large scale yellow and pink roses. The opposite Print #2 is a floral garden of light teal with yellow roses. Solid #3 and Solid #4 are pink and pale sage fern prints respectively.

It's important to have an accurate ¼" seam when sewing this quilt, and not a scant ¼" seam. Take the ¼" seam test before sewing.

Yardage

Finished Block Size 14" square	Wallhanging 2 x 2 = 4 total 46" x 46"	Lap 3 x 4 = 12 total 62" x 78"
Print #1	½ yd (1) 10½" strip cut into (1) 10½" x 20" (1) 6½" x 20" (2) 2½" strips Cut (1) in half	1 yd (1) 10½" strip Cut in half (1) 6½" strip Cut in half (5) 2½" strips Cut (1) in half
Print #2	½ yd (1) 10½" strip cut into (1) 10½" x 20" (1) 6½" x 20" (2) 2½" strips Cut (1) in half	1 yd (1) 10½" strip Cut in half (1) 6½" strip Cut in half (5) 2½" strips Cut (1) in half
Solid #3	½ yd (6) 2½" strips Cut (1) in half	1 yd (11) 2½" strips Cut (1) in half
Solid #4	½ yd (6) 2½" strips Cut (1) in half	1 yd (11) 2½" strips Cut (1) in half
Background Includes Framing Border Cornerstones	1 yd (12) 2½" strips Cut (7) in half (9) 2½" squares	1¾ yds (20) 2½" strips Cut (13) in half (20) 2½" squares
First Border	¾ yd (5) 4½" strips	1 yd (7) 4½" strips
Binding	½ yd (5) 3" strips	¾ yd (7) 3" strips
Batting	50" x 50"	70" x 86"
Backing	2¾ yds	4 yds

Paste Your Fabric Here (Print #1)

Paste Your Fabric Here (Print #2)

Paste Your Fabric Here (Solid #3)

Paste Your Fabric Here (Solid #4)

Paste Your Fabric Here (Background)

Paste Your Fabric Here (First Border)

Paste Your Fabric Here (Binding)

Twin	Full/Queen	King
3 x 5 = 15 total 64" x 96"	5 x 5 = 25 total 98" x 98"	6 x 6 = 36 total 114" x 114"
1¼ yds (1) 10½" strip Cut in half (1) 6½" strip Cut in half (6) 2½" strips Cut (1) in half	1¾ yds (2) 10½" strips Cut in half (2) 6½" strips Cut in half (10) 2½" strips Cut (2) in half	2⅓ yds (3) 10½" strips Cut in half (3) 6½" strips Cut in half (13) 2½" strips Cut (3) in half
1¼ yds (1) 10½" strip Cut in half (1) 6½" strip Cut in half (6) 2½" strips Cut (1) in half	1¾ yds (2) 10½" strips Cut in half (2) 6½" strips Cut in half (10) 2½" strips Cut (2) in half	2⅓ yds (3) 10½" strips Cut in half (3) 6½" strips Cut in half (13) 2½" strips Cut (3) in half
1¼ yds (14) 2½" strips Cut (1) in half	1¾ yds (24) 2½" strips Cut (2) in half	2 yds (27) 2½" strips Cut (3) in half
1¼ yds (14) 2½" strips Cut (1) in half	1¾ yds (24) 2½" strips Cut (2) in half	2 yds (27) 2½" strips Cut (3) in half
1¾ yds (22) 2½" strips Cut (13) in half (24) 2½" squares	2¼ yds (29) 2½" strips Cut (18) in half (36) 2½" squares	2¾ yds (36) 2½" strips Cut (20) in half (49) 2½" squares
1½ yds (8) 5½" strips	2 yds (9) 6½" strips	2⅓ yds (12) 6½" strips
¾ yd (8) 3" strips	1 yd (10) 3" strips	1¼ yd (12) 3" strips
72" x 104"	106" x 106"	120" x 120"
6 yds	9 yds	10 yds

Making Nine-Patches

1. Lay out 2½" half strips of #1 through #4 with 2½" half strips of Background. Turn right side up with cut edge at top. Place this many half strips in each stack.

Number of Half Strips	
Wallhanging	1
Lap	2
Twin	2
Full/Queen	4
King	5

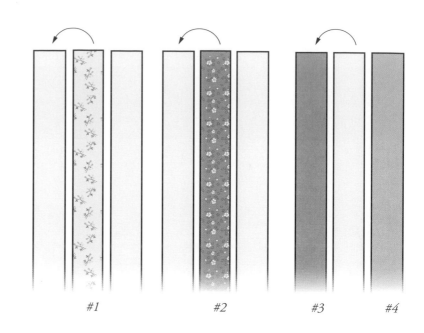

2. Sew all strips together.

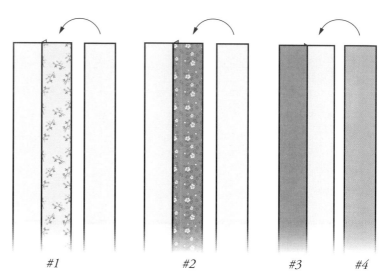

3. Press seams away from Background.

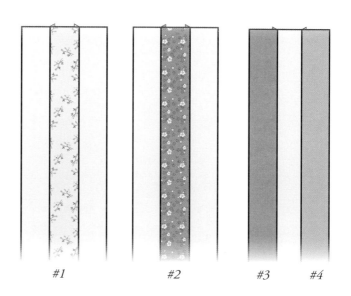

4. Cut each set into 2½" sections.

2½" Sections	
Wallhanging	4
Lap	12
Twin	15
Full/Queen	25
King	36

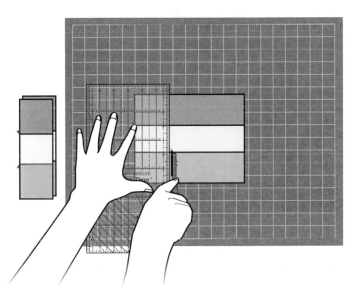

5. Lay out pieces to form a Nine-Patch.

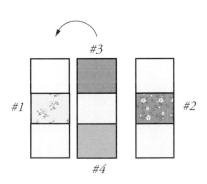

6. Lock seams, and assembly-line sew first two sets together.

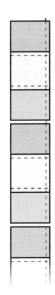

7. Assembly-line sew third set. Clip blocks apart.

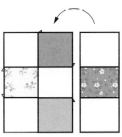

8. Press seams toward middle.

9. Measure size and record.

_____ Approx. 6½"

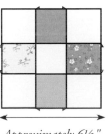

Approximately 6½"

Sewing Round One Sides

1. Stack Nine-Patches with Solid #3 on the left.

2. Place Solid #3 strips to left of Nine-Patches.

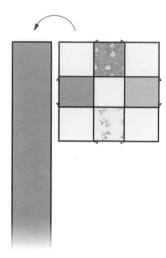

Solid #3

3. Flip Nine-Patches right sides together to strip and assembly-line sew.

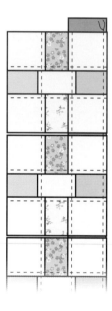

4. Cut strips even with Nine-Patches.

5. Turn over with strips on top. Set seam, open, and press seams away from Nine-Patches.

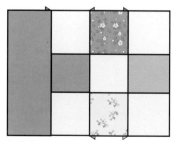

Solid #3

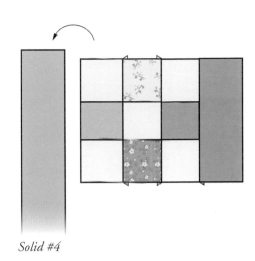

6. Stack Nine-Patches with Solid #4 on the left.

7. Place Solid #4 strips to left of Nine-Patches.

Solid #4

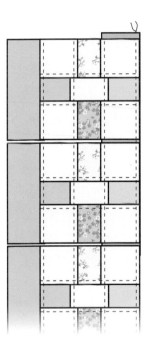

8. Flip Nine-Patches right sides together to strip and assembly-line sew.

9. Cut strips even with Nine-Patches.

10. Press seams away from Nine-Patches.

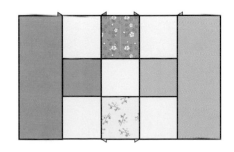

Sewing Round One Top and Bottom

1. Refer to measurement of Nine-Patches on page 155. If necessary, sliver trim 6½" strips of Prints #1 and #2 to size of Nine-Patches.

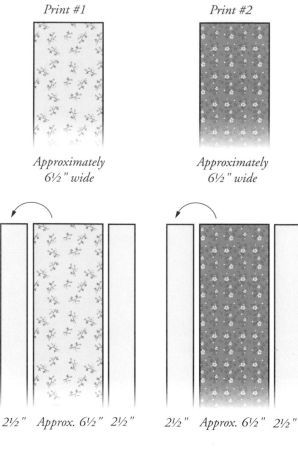

Print #1

Print #2

Approximately 6½" wide

Approximately 6½" wide

2. Lay out 6½" half strips of Prints #1 and #2, and half strips of 2½" Background. Place this many half strips in each stack.

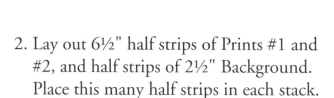

Number of Half Strips	
Wallhanging	1
Lap	2
Twin	2
Full/Queen	4
King	5

2½"   Approx. 6½"   2½"   *2½"   Approx. 6½"   2½"*

3. Sew 2½" Background strips to both sides of the Print #1 and #2 half strips. Clip blocks apart.

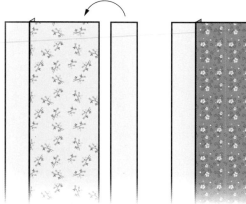

4. Press seams toward Prints.

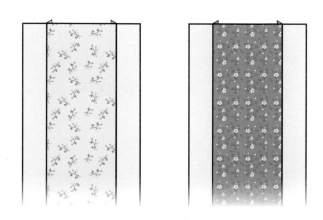

5. Cut 2½" sections from each Print fabric.

2½" Sections	
Wallhanging	4
Lap	12
Twin	15
Full/Queen	25
King	36

6. Assembly-line sew Print strips to both sides of Nine-Patches. Clip apart.

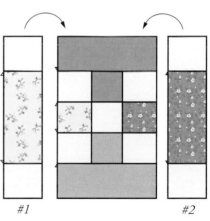

#1   #2

Optional: Pin locking seams.

7. Press seams away from Nine-Patches.

8. Measure size and record.

_____ Approx. 10½"

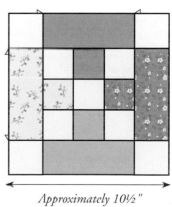

Approximately 10½"

Sewing Round Two

1. Assembly-line sew Solid #3 and #4 strips to both sides of Nine-Patches.

2. Cut strips even with Nine-Patches.

3. Press seams away from Nine-Patches.

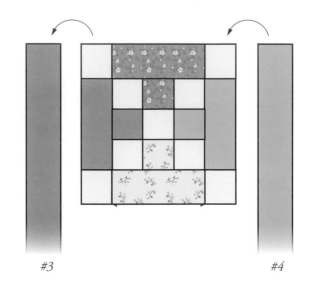

#3   *#4*

4. Refer to measurement of block on page 159, #8. If necessary, sliver trim 10½" strips of Prints #1 and #2 to size of block.

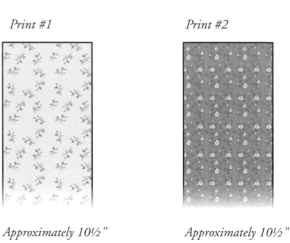

Print #1   *Print #2*

Approximately 10½"   *Approximately 10½"*

5. Lay out 10½" half strips of Prints #1 and #2, and half strips of 2½" Background. Place this many half strips in each stack.

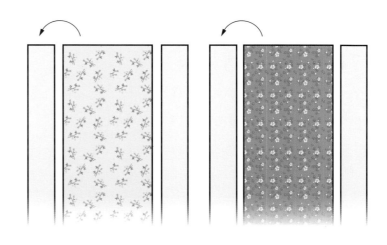

Number of Half Strips	
Wallhanging	1
Lap	2
Twin	2
Full/Queen	4
King	5

6. Sew Background strips to both sides of the Print half strips.

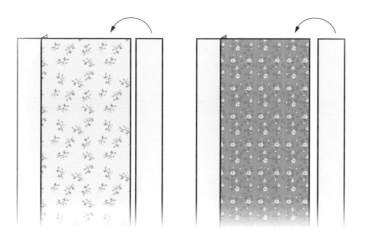

7. Press seams toward Prints.

8. Cut 2½" sections from each Print fabric.

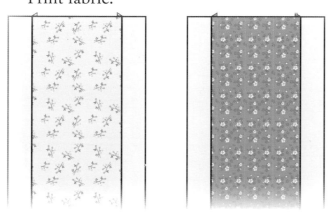

9. Assembly-line sew Print strips to both sides of Nine-Patches.

10. Press seams.

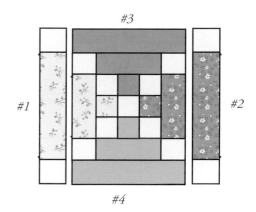

11. Measure size and record.

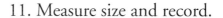

——————— Approx. 14½"

Lattice strips are cut this measurement.

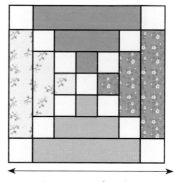

Approximately 14½"

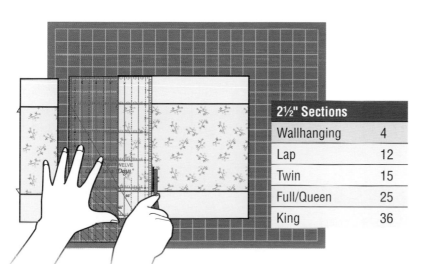

2½" Sections	
Wallhanging	4
Lap	12
Twin	15
Full/Queen	25
King	36

Sewing Top Together

1. Cut 2½" strips x size of block for Lattice. Cut Lattice strips as indicated on chart on right.

2. Lay out blocks **with #1 Print in upper left corner.** Place appropriate Lattice between blocks.

3. Place 2½" Background Cornerstones between blocks.

4. Assembly-line sew vertical rows of quilt top together.

5. Sew remaining rows, pushing seams toward Lattice so every seam locks.

6. Sew 2½" Background Border and outside Border.

7. Turn to **Finishing Instructions** on page 226.

Lattice Strips	Print #1	Print #2	Solid #3	Solid #4
Wallhanging	3	3	3	3
Lap	8	8	8	7
Twin	10	10	9	9
Full/Queen	15	15	15	15
King	21	21	21	21

Cornerstones	
Wallhanging	9
Lap	20
Twin	24
Full/Queen	36
King	49

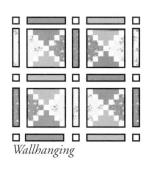

Wallhanging

Lap

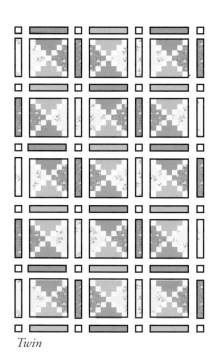

Twin

Pieced and quilted by Teresa Varnes *46" x 46"*

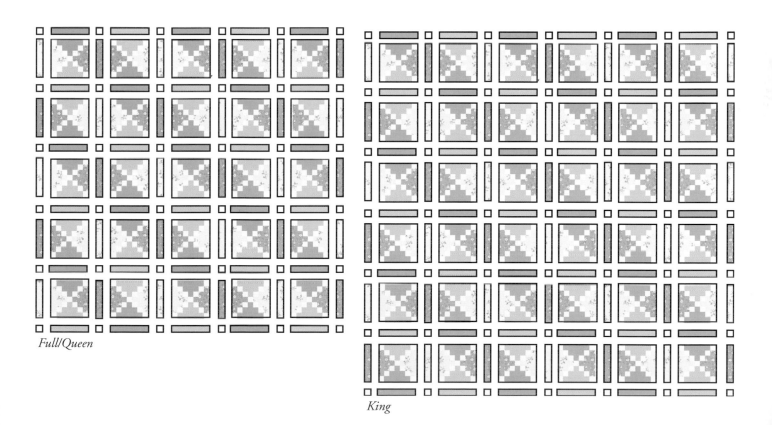

Full/Queen

King

Early Firecracker Quilt

Born on the 3rd of July in 1945, Mother always told me I popped too soon. I love red, white and blue birthdays! It's just a flag waving kind of day for love of land and countrymen.

Give me a flag, and I'll wave it high. Sharing coffee and apple pie with good friend Sue Bouchard, I am thankful for the Freedom my country has given me. Draping red, white and blue quilts over my railing at my log home in Julian, California, is a perfect way to display patriotism.

Eleanor Burns for President

Star Template
for
Free Motion Quilting

Optional
Use template as pattern for
appliquéd star.

In her scrappy patriotic quilt, Eleanor used
traditional tones of red, white and blue.
This striking lap robe boasts quilted stars to
complete the patriotic mood.

Pieced by Eleanor Burns
Quilted by Carol Selepec
49" x 57"

Finished Block Size	Lap Robe
8" square	4 x 5 = 20 total 49" x 57"

Background	1⅓ yds
	(4) 2½" strips cut into
	      (20) 2½" x 6½" pieces
	(3) 5½" strips cut into
	      (20) 5½" squares

Framing Border	(6) 3" strips
Prints	**Red Prints** (5) different ¼ yd pieces Cut from each piece (4) 2½" x 6½" pieces (2) 5½" squares **Blue Prints** (5) different ¼ yd pieces Cut from each piece (4) 2½" x 6½" pieces (2) 5½" squares
Border	1¼ yds (7) 6" strips
Binding	⅔ yd (7) 3" strips
Backing	3½ yds
Batting	56" x 64"

Paste Your Fabric Here

Red Print	Blue Print
Red Print	Blue Print
Red Print	Blue Print
Red Print	Blue Print
Red Print	Blue Print

Paste Your Fabric Here

How to Select Your Fabric

Select a variety of red and blue prints in similar values and varying scales, plus one background fabric. Use the same background for the framing border and one of the blue prints for the border.

How about a Fourth of July autograph party?
Cut twenty blocks ahead of time, and package each block individually for party participants.

Making Ten Red Stripe Blocks

Make ten blocks with red stripes and blue corners, and ten blocks with blue stripes and red corners.

6. Cut 5½" squares Background in half on one diagonal.

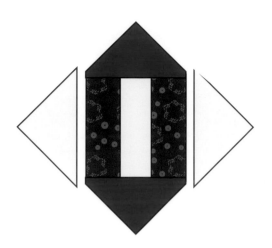

1. Stack 2½" x 6½" strips of red prints and Background, and sew together with accurate ¼" seam.

2. Press seams toward red.

7. Sew triangles to strip patch.

8. Press seams toward triangles.

3. Cut 5½" squares blue print fabric in half on one diagonal.

4. Sew triangles to strip patch.

5. Press seams toward triangles. Trim tips.

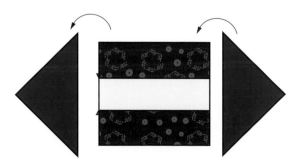

Making Ten Blue Stripe Blocks

1. Stack sets of blue strips and Background and sew together with accurate ¼" seam.

2. Press seams toward blue.

3. Cut 5½" squares red print fabric in half on one diagonal.

4. Sew triangles to strip patch.

5. Press seams toward triangles. Trim tips.

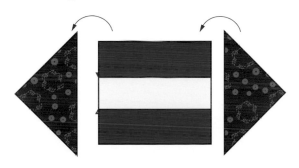

6. Cut 5½" squares Background in half on one diagonal.

7. Sew triangles to strip patch.

8. Press seams toward triangles.

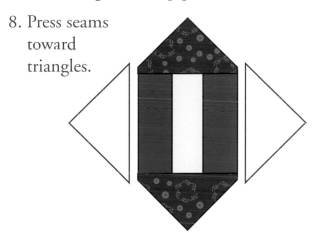

9. Square up all patches to the same size, approximately 8¾".

10. Sign blocks with permanent marking pen.

11. Lay out blocks in five rows with four blocks across. Alternate between red stripes and blue stripes.

12. Sew top together.

13. Turn to **Finishing Instructions** on page 226.

14. Make star template and trace on Background squares.

15. Free motion quilt Stars in Background spaces.

Autograph Quilt

When students ask, I autograph anything for them – books, cups, sewing machines, fabric scraps, stripper bags, fans – Whatever! I have a vision of an archeological dig in a thousand years. The researcher digs through all that old stuff, and shouts, "Who is Eleanor Burns anyway?"

The most popular items I autograph are my books. Another popular item is my cloth bag that says, "Eleanor Burns made a stripper out of me", with my signature strip throwing pose. As a spokesperson for Elna, I was quite flattered to sign 1,000 Quilter's Dreams. I personally bought two signature sewing machines for my granddaughters. They are both very bright, but I haven't been able to teach them to sew. Maybe it's because they are Labradors!

For my 25th silver anniversary, Elna is again honoring me with a signature Quilter's Dream, with the added bonus of a red, blue, and silver quilt. Maybe the girls will learn to sew on this new one.

March 6, 2003

Eleanor Burns
Quilt in a Day
1955 Diamond Street
San Marcos, CA 92069

Dear Eleanor,

Congratulations on your Silver Anniversary.

The first quilting book I ever purchased was "Quilt in a Day Log Cabin". It was the second quilt I ever made. I wish I could express my gratitude for information and inspiration you have given me over the years.

Here's hoping you enjoy another 25 years of good health and success.

Sincerely,

Dear Eleanor,
Congratu
25th Anniver
I first
1985 at the I
You made q
like so m
nice. I b
three boo
a shelf of y
quilt boo
in my l
class and
changed
Tod

about quiltmaking as I
was in the very
beginning.
Thank you from the
bottom of my heart for
changing my life for
the better. I will never
forget you.

Sincerely,
Patricia L. Cassell

2549 Golden Rain Rd #4
Walnut Creek, Ca. 94595
www.sewbusy 2549 @ aTTbi.com

Rita R

LilyJane Moody

Shirley Riley
Oceanside, California
Quilters with Loving Hands
Quilt In A Day 2003

Betty

Peggy Lee Caballero

Bravo!

Sharon Kazycki

When students were asked to make autograph blocks for my 25th Anniversary Celebration quilt, a total of 712 blocks arrived, representing every state in the Union. Teresa Varnes spent days sewing the huge quilt together, finishing it at 9' x 48', the size of six king size quilts. Neta Virgin was gracious enough to quilt it on her long arm quilting machine. The finishing touch required thirty-five selvage to selvage binding strips. This spectacular quilt debuted in April, 2003, draped over our huge tent in Paducah, Kentucky during the AQS show.

The contributed blocks are all special to me. Mothers and daughters, husbands and wives, friends mailed them in, many with complimentary letters and stories about how we met. Some blocks were made with authentic 1930's fabric, collected from ancestors. One of my favorite blocks was the one sewn in red thread, my signature color for my television viewers.

My plan now is to have the world's largest sleepover under one quilt!

One Autograph Block

(2) 2½" x 6½"   strips 1930's reproduction fabric
(1) 2½" x 6½"   strip muslin
(1) 5½" x 5½"   reproduction fabric
(1) 5½" x 5½"   muslin

1. Sew strips together with accurate ¼" seam.

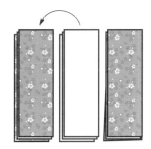

2. Press seams toward dark.

3. Cut 5½" square reproduction fabric in half on one diagonal.

4. Sew triangles to strip patch.

5. Press seams toward triangles. Trim tips.

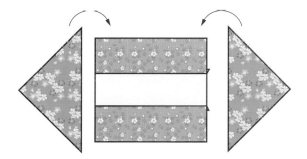

6. Cut 5½" square muslin in half on one diagonal.

7. Sew triangles to strip patch.

8. Press seams toward triangles.

9. **Do not square up patch.** Autographed patches will be squared to same size.

10. Sign block with permanent marking pen.

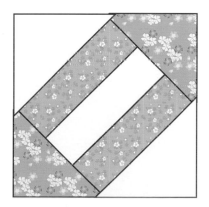

You are welcome to photocopy this pattern for your friends to make their own autograph blocks.

Candy Jar Quilt

For this "grandma's candy jar" quilt, Eleanor Burns and Teresa Varnes teamed up and used reproduction 30's fabrics. They chose to leave the quilt unsigned, giving the effect of old fashioned hard candy pieces. Yummy!

Pieced by Eleanor Burns
Quilted by Teresa Varnes
54" x 78"

Yardage

Finished Block Size 8" square	Lap Robe 5 x 8 = 40 total 54" x 78"
Background	2¼ yds (10) 2½" strips (6) 5½" strips cut into (40) 5½" squares
Framing Border	(6) 3" strips
Prints	(10) different ¼ yd pieces Cut from each piece (1) 2½" strip (4) 5½" squares
Border	1¼ yds (7) 6" strips
Binding	⅔ yd (7) 3" strips
Backing	4 yds
Batting	60" x 84"

Paste Your Fabric Here

Paste Your Fabric Here

How to Select Your Fabric

Select a variety of prints in different scales, or read solid from a distance, plus a neutral Background.

Without signatures, the colorful blocks look like wrapped hard candy. Perfect for a Reunion Quilt, single names could be signed on Block A, and couples or families on Block B.

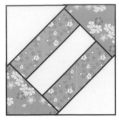

Block A *Block B*

Sewing Strips

1. Cut 2½" strips in half on fold. Turn right side up. Stack variety of strips.

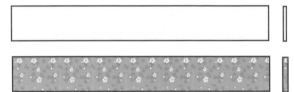

Stack selvage on left edge.

2. Layer cut half strips into three pieces approximately 7" long. Leave in three separate stacks.

3. Arrange 7" strips for Block A and Block B.

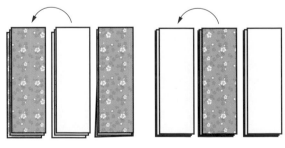

Block A *Block B*

4. Assembly-line sew, carefully keeping strips in order. Set seams with dark on top, open, and press seams toward dark.

Do not clip connecting threads.

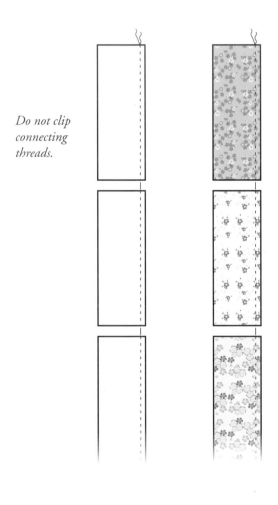

Block A *Block B*

5. Assembly-line sew remaining strips.

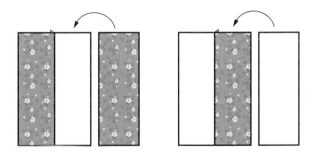

6. Set seams, and press toward dark.

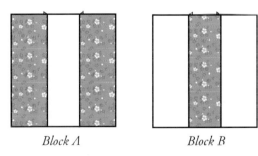

Block A   *Block B*

7. Measure width of pressed block.

Approximately 6½"

8. Square block into that length with 12½" Square Up ruler.

Approximately 6½"

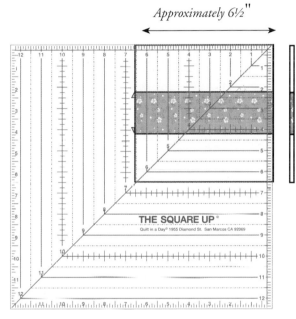

Line up ruler's diagonal line on opposite corners.

Finishing Twenty Block A

1. Layer cut twenty 5½" print squares on one diagonal.

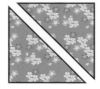

Keep in two separate stacks.

2. Stack strip patches with print triangles. Flip patch right sides together to triangle, and center. Sew with bias stretch of triangle on bottom.

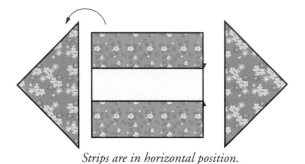

Strips are in horizontal position.

3. Sew second print triangle.

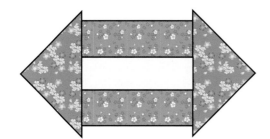

4. Set seams with triangles on top, open, and press seams toward triangles.

5. Trim tips even with strip patch.

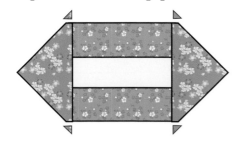

6. Layer cut 5½" Background squares on one diagonal.

7. Stack strip patches with Background triangles. Flip patch right sides together to triangles, center, and sew.

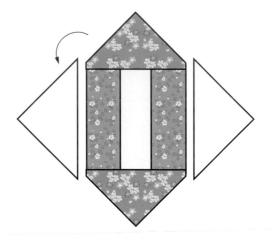

8. Set seams with triangles on top, open, and press seams toward triangles.

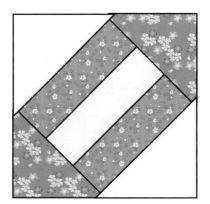

Finishing Twenty Block B

1. Layer cut twenty 5½" print squares on one diagonal.

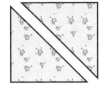

Keep in two separate stacks.

2. Stack strip patches with print triangles. Flip patch right sides together to triangle, and center. Sew with bias stretch of triangle on bottom.

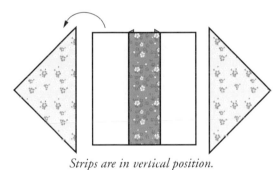

Strips are in vertical position.

3. Sew second print triangle.

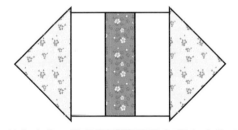

4. Set seams with triangles on top, open, and press seams toward triangles.

5. Trim tips even with strip patch.

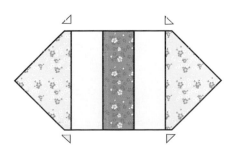

6. Layer cut 5½" Background squares on one diagonal.

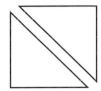

7. Stack strip patches with Background triangles. Flip patch right sides together to triangles, center, and sew.

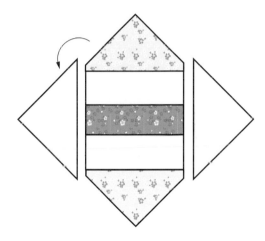

8. Set seams with triangles on top, open, and press seams toward triangles.

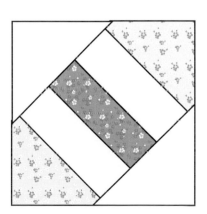

9. Place 12½" Square Up's diagonal line down center of strips. Place ¼" line on seams.

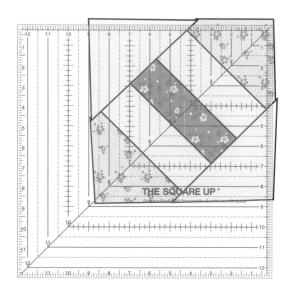

10. Trim on two sides. Turn and trim remaining two sides.

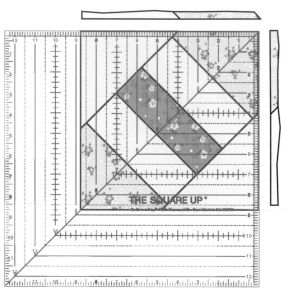

Square to approximately 8¾".

11. Leave ¼" seams on all four sides.

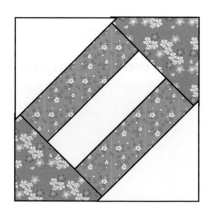

Sewing Top Together

1. Lay out Block A in Row One with five blocks across.

2. Lay out Block B in Row Two.

3. Repeat these two rows in five blocks across, and eight blocks down.

4. Flip second vertical row right sides together to first vertical row. Assembly-line sew all vertical rows.

5. Sew remaining rows, pushing seams in opposite directions.

6. Follow **Finishing Instructions** on page 226.

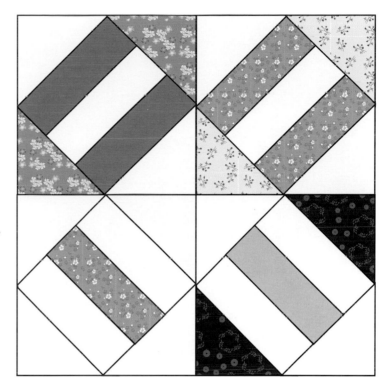

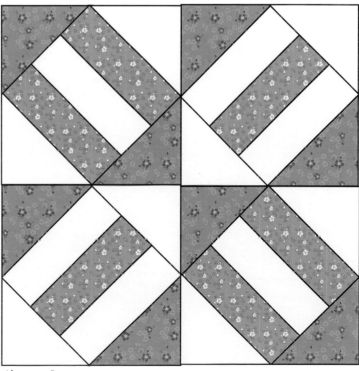

Alternate Layout

Fabric Gal Quilt

From the beginning, the Quilt in a Day store has been a favorite project of mine. I love to get in there and fondle all that new fabric! Imagine my excitement when Selim Benardete of Benartex Fabrics, asked me to collaborate on a fabric line. My sister Patricia, with her artistic eye, was a great help in designing the first line, Anniversary Florals. Teamed with my book, *Grandmother's Garden,* the first line was a hit! Rainbow Florals followed, featured in *Delectable Mountains Quilt.* Yours Truly is my favorite line, featured in *Still Stripping* to celebrate 25 years of quilting.

17, 1999

Eleanor:

ratulations! As th
..., I am pleased
...ed the winner of
...rd at Quilt Marke

...s award is given an
...rumental in furthe
...omplishments hav
...oday. You are bei
...ilters and for your
...oes not have to tak
...d easy and fun. Y
quilt shops everywhere still are
Quilt in a Day method are instantly "hooked" on quilting
continue making them. And that, of course, to the delight and benefit
of all quilt stores everywhere, means they will need to buy more fabric!

Congratulations, Eleanor— you deserve this recognition for all you
...done for quilting. I look forward to seeing what new ground you
...k as we enter the 21st century and the third millennium!

INTERNATIONAL QUILT MARKET

QUILT EXPO

EUROPEAN QUILT MARKET

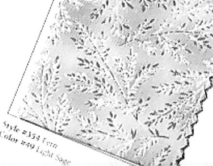

Style #350
Remembrance
Color #60
Creme Purple

Style #354 Fern
Color #49 Sage

Style #354 Fern
Color #49 Light Sage

Anniversary F[...]
by Eleanor Burns

Yours Truly
by Eleanor Burns

Style #356 Circles and Flowers
Color #10 Crème Purple

Style #352 Floral Garden
Color #60 Lilac Purple

Style #355 Petite Roses
Color #20 Lilac Gold

Style #355
Petite Roses
Color #40
Sage Purple

Style #350 Remembrance
Color #66 Purple

Fabric Selection

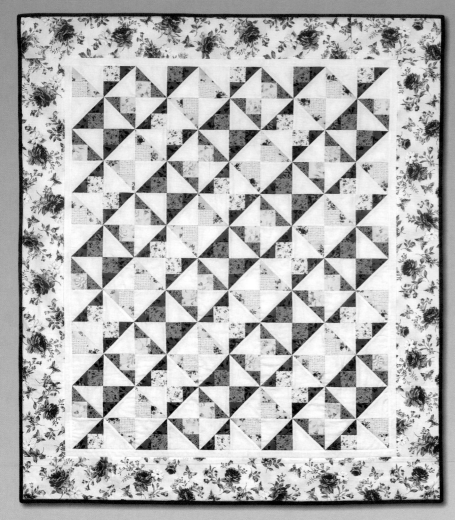

Top
Using a variety of fabrics from Rainbow Florals, Loretta created a lovely lap robe in pastel colors, framed with a large-scale rose print.

Pieced by Loretta Smith
Quilted by Teresa Varnes
53" x 61"

Bottom Left
How many spinners can you count? Sue selected crayon box colors for her bright and cheerful wallhanging. Bound with cherry red, it is a kid pleaser!

Pieced by Sue Bouchard
Quilted by Amie Potter
42" x 42"

Bottom Right
Teresa achieved a soft and delicate tone for her wallhanging, using Yours Truly fabrics in a bouquet of pastels.

Pieced and Quilted by
Teresa Varnes
42" x 42"

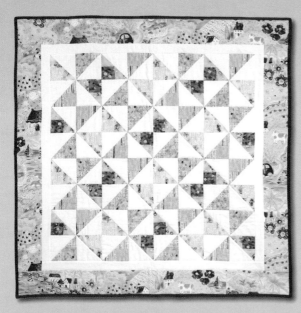

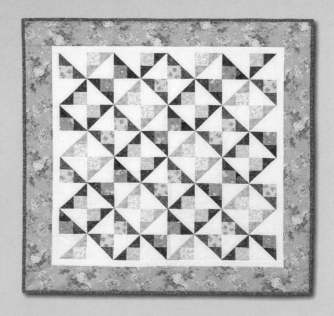

Yours Truly

Fabrics by

BENARTEX
INCORPORATED

Background
First Border

241-07

First
Medium

352-49

First
Dark
Second
Border

354-44

Second
Medium

355-26

Second
Dark

350-66

Third
Medium

354-84

Third
Dark

352-48

Fourth
Medium

355-01

Fourth
Dark

354-26

For a bold and beautiful look, Loretta framed her quilt in deep sage. She used coordinating Yours Truly fabrics on a crisp white background for a stunning effect.

53" x 61"

Pieced by Loretta Smith
Quilted by Teresa Varnes

How to Select Your Fabric

Select one Background and four different colors of fabrics. From each color, chose two values - a medium and a dark in different scales of prints. Use Background for the First Border, one of the mediums for Second Border, and one of the darks for Third Border.

In the sample quilt, fern prints reading solid from a distance are complimented with softer petite rose prints. The rich deep fern print in the Third Border pulls the block fabrics together.

Fat quarters are perfect for Fabric Gal blocks. Just cut twice as many half strips as listed full strips. You can get seven half strips per fat quarter equal to 3½ full strips.

185

Yardage

Finished Block Size 8" square	Wallhanging 4 x 4 =16 total 40" x 40"	Lap 5 x 6 = 30 total 52" x 60"
Light Background	¾ yd (5) 4½" strips cut into (32) 4½" x 5½" rectangles	1¼ yds (9) 4½" strips cut into (60) 4½" x 5½" rectangles
Four Different Mediums	⅛ yd of each (1) 2½" strip from each	¼ yd of each (2) 2½" strips from each
Four Coordinating Darks	⅛ yd of each (1) 3½" strip from each	¼ yd of each (2) 3½" strips from each
First Border	¼ yd (4) 1½" strips	⅓ yd (5) 1½" strips
Second Border	⅝ yd (4) 4½" strips	1⅛ yds (6) 6" strips
Third Border		
Binding	½ yd (5) 3" strips	⅝ yd (6) 3" strips
Backing	1¼ yds	3¾ yds
Batting	46" x 46"	58" x 66"

Paste Your Fabric Here

Twin	Full/Queen	King
6 x 10 = 60 total 72" x 104"	8 x 10 = 80 total 88" x 104"	10 x 10 = 100 total 104" x 104"
2½ yds (18) 4½" strips cut into (120) 4½" x 5½" rectangles	3 yds (23) 4½" strips cut into (160) 4½" x 5½" rectangles	4 yds (29) 4½" strips cut into (200) 4½" x 5½" rectangles
⅓ yd of each (4) 2½" strips from each	½ yd of each (5) 2½" strips from each	⅝ yd of each (7) 2½" strips from each
½ yd of each (4) 3½" strips from each	⅔ yd of each (5) 3½" strips from each	¾ yd of each (7) 3½" strips from each
⅝ yd (7) 2½" strips	⅔ yd (8) 2½" strips	⅔ yd (8) 2½" strips
1¼ yds (7) 5½" strips	1½ yds (9) 5½" strips	1½ yds (9) 5½" strips
2 yds (9) 7½" strips	2¼ yds (10) 7½" strips	2½ yds (11) 7½" strips
1 yd (9) 3" strips	1 yd (10) 3" strips	1⅛ yds (11) 3" strips
6 yds	8 yds	9 yds
80" x 112"	98" x 114"	114" x 114"

Making Double Patches

Two patches are made at a time from two different widths of strips.

1. Cut strips in half on fold. Stack with cut edge at top.

2. Sew one 2½" medium strip right sides together to one coordinating 3½" dark strip.

3. Set seam with 3½" strip on top, open, and press against seam.

4. Measure width of strip. It should measure 5½". If necessary, adjust seam. Repeat for all pairs.

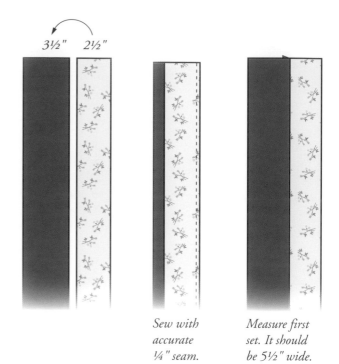

Sew with accurate ¼" seam.

Measure first set. It should be 5½" wide.

5. Lay first strip right side up on gridded cutting mat with 2½" strip across top. Place **matching strip** right sides together to it with 3½" strip across top. **Seams do not meet.** Line up strips with grid.

6. Square left end. Cut 2½" pairs from each set of colors. Use 6" x 12" ruler or Shape Cut™. Stack on spare ruler to carry to sewing area.

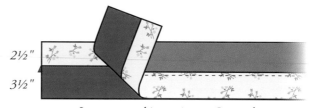

Lay out matching strip sets. Seams do not meet.

2½" Pairs of Each Set	
Wallhanging	8
Lap	15
Twin	30
Full/Queen	40
King	50

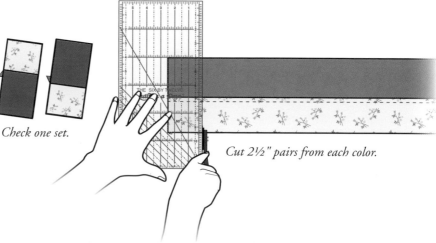

Check one set.

Cut 2½" pairs from each color.

7. Assembly-line sew.

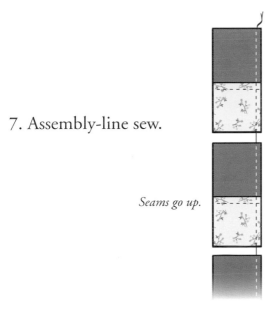

Seams go up.

8. Fold in half, and clip seam in middle **to** the stitching.

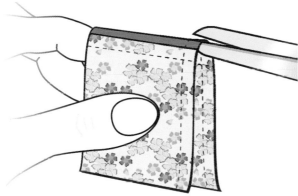

9. From right side, press into one square. Turn, and press into opposite square.

10. Check on wrong side.

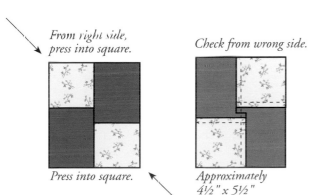

From right side, press into square.

Check from wrong side.

Press into square.

Approximately 4½" x 5½"

11. Turn patch vertically wrong side up. Place 45° diagonal line on 6½" Triangle Square Up ruler on **long side**. Line up ruler's edge on stitched point of medium square and top left edge of patch. See circles.

Ruler's edge is at point.

12. **Draw a line that will be your sewing line.**

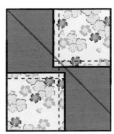

Ruler crosses stitches

13. Turn the patch. With ruler, draw another sewing line across the point of the other medium square.

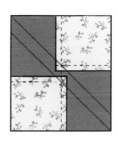

14. Layer patches right sides together with 4½" x 5½" Background rectangles for each set. Pin.

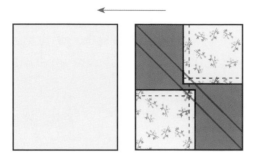

15. Use center needle position and open toe foot. Assembly-line sew on left line indicated by arrow. Turn and assembly-line sew on remaining line. Hold seams flat with stiletto.

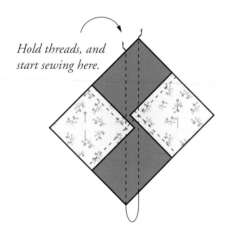

Hold threads, and start sewing here.

16. Cut between the lines.

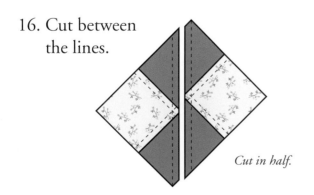

Cut in half.

17. Set seams with Background on top.

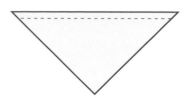

18. Open, and press seam to Background.

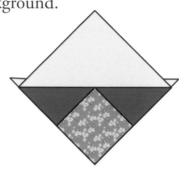

19. Trim tips.

20. The patch should measure approximately 4½" square. Sliver trim if necessary.

Sewing Blocks Together

1. Lay out block. Stack identical patches in each stack.

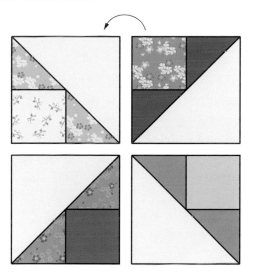

Patches in Each Stack	
Wallhanging	16
Lap	30
Twin	60
Full/Queen	80
King	100

2. Flip patches on right to patches on left, right sides together.

3. Pin or wiggle-match seams.

4. Assembly-line sew stacks. Leave a gap between blocks for easy separating.

5. Clip apart at the gap between blocks.

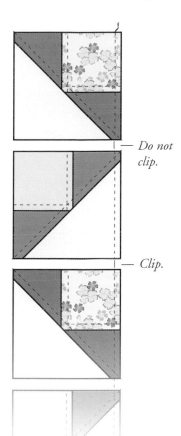

Do not clip.

Clip.

6. Open and flip the patches right side together. **Push top seam upward and underneath seam downward.** Wiggle-match or pin center seams.

7. Assembly-line sew the blocks.

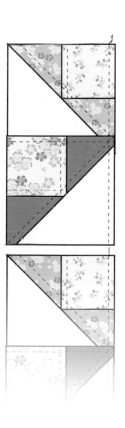

8. At the center seam, cut the first stitch with scissors. See circle.

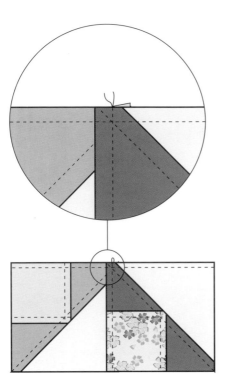

10. Open center seams and push down flat to form a tiny pinwheel.

11. Press new seams clockwise around the block.

12. You may "sliver trim" to square them consistently, but it is not necessary if they are all close in size.

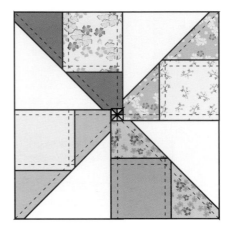

9. Remove three vertical stitches at center on both sides with stiletto or seam ripper.

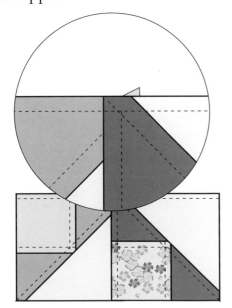

Sewing Top Together

1. Lay out blocks. The pattern is formed by turning blocks in only two directions. Alternate between these two.

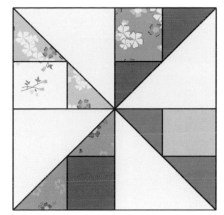 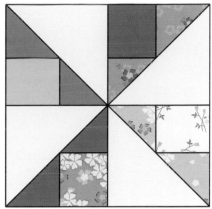

Blocks Across and Down		
Wallhanging	4	4
Lap	5	6
Twin	6	10
Full/Queen	8	10
King	10	10

2. Assembly-line sew vertical rows together.

3. Sew horizontal rows. Push the seams between blocks in opposite directions.

4. Press the quilt first on the wrong side, then on the right side.

5. If necessary, straighten the outside edges without removing ¼" seam allowances.

6. Add Borders.

7. Turn to **Finishing Instructions** on page 226.

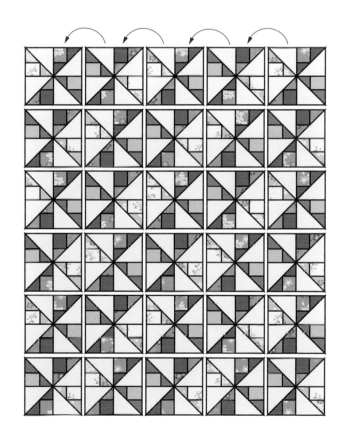

Crossing Pathways Quilt

It's always a pleasant surprise to be honored for your work. For me, it's confirmation that I'm using the God given talents I have been blessed with. "Women of Merit" was one such award, plus numerous awards for quality books and rulers. "Woman in Business Advocate of the Year" confirms that I have helped others like myself survive.

The one I am most proud of is the 1999 Michael Kile Lifetime Achievement Award from the Quilt Market Advisory board. They stated, "Once students make a Quilt in a Day quilt, they are instantly hooked. And that, of course, to the delight and benefit of all quilt stores everywhere, means they will need to buy more fabric!".

SOUTHERN CRAFT MANUFACTURERS

PCM
Award of Excellence

PRESENTED TO

QUILT IN A DAY INC.

FOR

1993 QUILTERS' ALMANAC

1991

This Certificate is Presented to

Quilt in a Day

In Sincere Appreciation for

Silver Sponsorship

Road to California 2002

Eleanor Burns
of
Quilt In A Day

1999 Winner
of the
**Michael Kile
Award of Achievement**

*Honoring commitment
to creativity and excellence
in the quilting industry*

International Quilt Market
Houston, Texas
October, 1999

ELEANOR A. BURNS

Has Been Selected
As An

Honored Member
in the

NATIONAL DIRECTORY
of
WHO'S WHO
IN EXECUTIVES & PROFESSIONALS

FOR THE

1993-1994 Edition

Fabric Selection

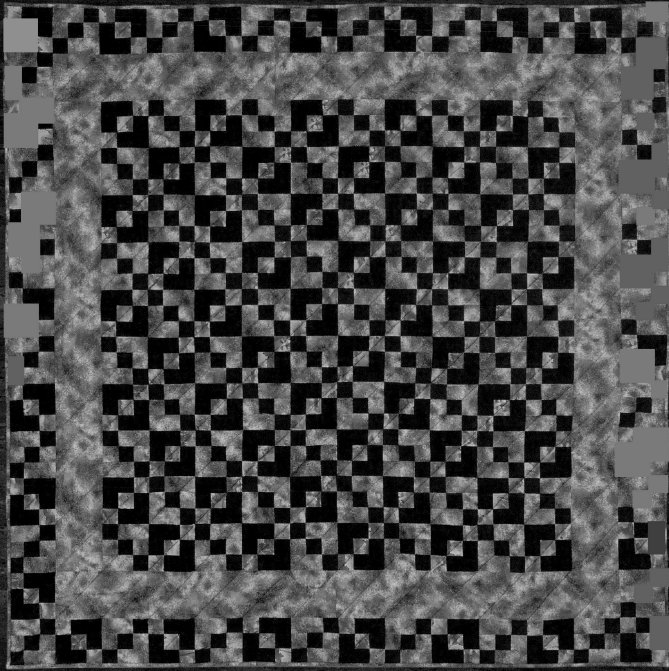

84" x 84"

For a spirited quilt, Linda used black and turquoise to make her pathways of rust cross through her quilt. She duplicated the pattern blocks for a stunning border.

Pieced and Quilted by Linda McKenna

Pieced by Amber Varnes
Quilted by Amie Potter

60" x 72"

Block One
Dark Fabric A

350-84

Block One
Light Fabric B

Inside
Border

355-30

Block Two
Light Medium
Fabric C

356-05

Block Two
Dark Medium
Fabric D

352-84

How to Select Your Fabric

Select a dark Fabric A and light Fabric B for Block One, and a light medium Fabric C and dark medium Fabric D for Block Two. The Inside Border is the same light used in Block One. Vary scales of prints, as one large scale, one medium scale, one small scale, and one that reads solid. The chains are dark Fabric A and light medium Fabric C.

In the sample quilt, Block One is large scale deep teal roses paired with a light print of petite roses. Block Two is a medium blue floral garden fabric paired with a light medium yellow fabric graced with bundles of flowers and circles.

Yardage

Finished Block Size 6" square	Wallhanging 4 x 4 = 16 total for top plus 28 for border 48" x 48"	Lap 6 x 8 = 48 total for top plus 40 for border 60" x 72"
Dark Fabric A	½ yd (5) 2½" strips cut in half	¾ yd (9) 2½" strips cut in half
Light Fabric B	¾ yd (3) 2½" strips cut in half (3) 4½" strips cut in half	1⅓ yds (6) 2½" strips cut in half (6) 4½" strips cut in half
Inside Border	1 yd (4) 6½" strips	1 yd (5) 6½" strips
Light Medium Fabric C	½ yd (5) 2½" strips cut in half	¾ yd (9) 2½" strips cut in half
Dark Medium Fabric D	¾ yd (3) 2½" strips cut in half (3) 4½" strips cut in half	1⅓ yds (6) 2½" strips cut in half (6) 4½" strips cut in half
Binding	½ yd (5) 3" strips	⅔ yd (7) 3" strips
Backing	3⅓ yds	4⅓ yds
Batting	54" x 54"	68" x 80"

Paste Your Fabric Here

Paste Your Fabric Here

Paste Your Fabric Here

Paste Your Fabric Here

Paste Your Fabric Here

This quilt gets rave reviews. Rich forest green squares prance across the large scale floral meadow.

Pieced by Linda Fornaca
Quilted by Amie Potter
60" x 72"

Twin	Full/Queen	King
8 x 12 = 96 total for top plus 52 for border 72" x 96"	10 x 14 = 140 total for top plus 60 for border 84" x 108"	14 x 14 = 196 total for top plus 68 for border 108" x 108"
1⅛ yds (15) 2½" strips cut in half	1¾ yds (20) 2½" strips cut in half	2 yds (26) 2½" strips cut in half
2⅛ yds (10) 2½" strips cut in half (10) 4½" strips cut in half	2¾ yds (13) 2½" strips cut in half (13) 4½" strips cut in half	3½ yds (17) 2½" strips cut in half (17) 4½" strips cut in half
1½ yds (7) 6½" strips	1⅔ yds (8) 6½" strips	2 yds (10) 6½" strips
1⅛ yds (15) 2½" strips cut in half	1¾ yds (20) 2½" strips cut in half	2 yds (25) 2½" strips cut in half
2⅛ yds (10) 2½" strips cut in half (10) 4½" strips cut in half	2¾ yds (13) 2½" strips cut in half (13) 4½" strips cut in half	3½ yds (17) 2½" strips cut in half (17) 4½" strips cut in half
⅞ yd (9) 3" strips	1 yd (10) 3" strips	1⅛ yds (12) 3" strips
6 yds	7½ yds	10 yds
80" x 104"	90" x 116"	116" x 116"

Making Block One

These instructions are enough for inside of quilt and pieced border.

 Making Two Piece Sections

You need two for each block.

1. Stack 2½" Fabric A half strips with 4½" Fabric B half strips right side up with cut edges at top.

Number of Half Strips	
Wallhanging	6
Lap	12
Twin	20
Full/Queen	26
King	34

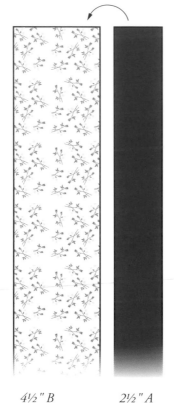

2. Flip Fabric A onto Fabric B. Assembly-line sew with accurate ¼" seam and 15 stitches per inch, or 2.0 on computerized machine.

4½" B   *2½" A*

3. Set seams with Fabric A on top. Open, and press seam toward Fabric A.

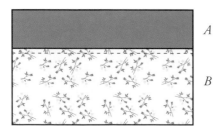

A

B

 Making Three Piece Sections

You need one for each block.

1. Make two stacks of 2½" Fabric B half strips with 2½" Fabric A half strips.

Number of Half Strips	
Wallhanging	3
Lap	6
Twin	10
Full/Queen	13
King	17

2. Assembly-line sew Fabric A to Fabric B. Set seam with Fabric A on top. Open, and press seam toward Fabric A.

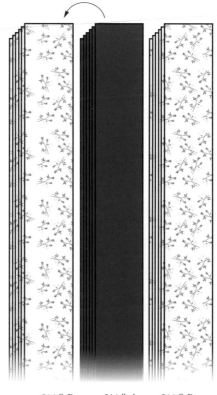

2½" B   *2½" A*   *2½" B*

3. Assembly-line sew Fabric B to Fabric B/A. Set seam with Fabric A on top. Open, and press seam toward Fabric A.

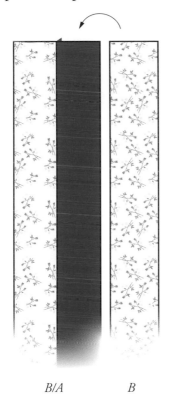

B/A   B

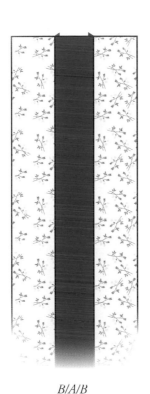

B/A/B

Sewing Block One Together

1. Place one Three Piece Section on cutting mat right side up. Place Two Piece Section right sides together to first. **Narrow strip A is across top.** Lock seam.

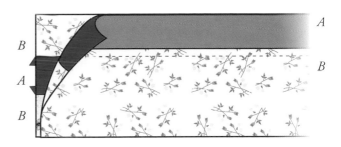

2. Square left end. Cut into 2½" sections. Use 6" x 12" ruler or Shape Cut. Leave paired together.

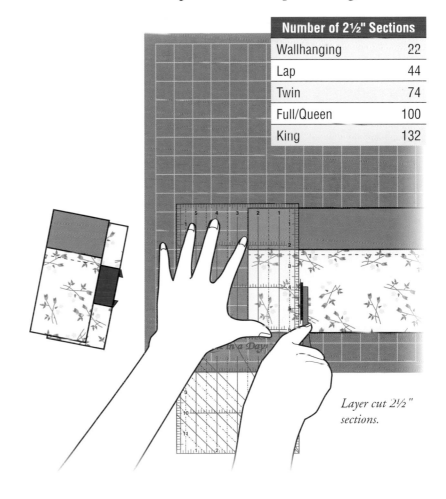

Number of 2½" Sections	
Wallhanging	22
Lap	44
Twin	74
Full/Queen	100
King	132

Layer cut 2½" sections.

3. Assembly-line sew pairs together. Do not press.

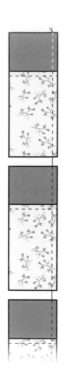

5. Assembly-line sew together.

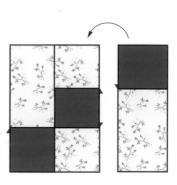

4. Place remaining Two Piece Sections on cutting mat. Layer cut into 2½" sections.

Number of 2½" Sections	
Wallhanging	22
Lap	44
Twin	74
Full/Queen	100
King	132

Cut 2½" sections.

6. From wrong side, press seams in one direction.

7. Sliver trim outside edges if necessary.

Press seams in one direction.

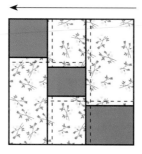

Making Block Two

Block Two is sewn differently than Block One.

 Making Two Piece Sections

1. Stack 2½" Fabric C half strips with 4½" Fabric D half strips right side up with cut edges at top.

Number of Half Strips	
Wallhanging	6
Lap	12
Twin	20
Full/Queen	26
King	34

2. Flip Fabric C onto Fabric D. Assembly-line sew.

4½" D   2½" C

3. Set seams with Fabric D on top. Open, and press seam toward Fabric D.

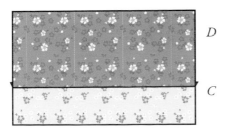

D

C

Making Three Piece Sections

1. Make two stacks of 2½" Fabric D half strips with 2½" Fabric C half strips.

Number of Half Strips	
Wallhanging	3
Lap	6
Twin	10
Full/Queen	13
King	17

2. Assembly-line sew Fabric C to Fabric D. Set seam with Fabric D on top. Open, and press seam toward Fabric D.

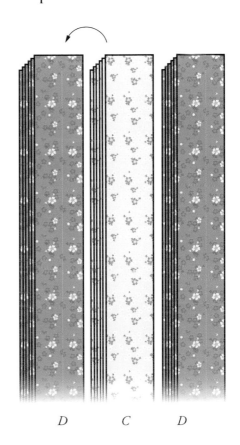

D   C   D

3. Assembly-line sew Fabric D to Fabric D/C. Set seam with Fabric D on top. Open, and press seam toward Fabric D.

D/C   *D*

D/C/D

Sewing Block Two Together

1. Place one Three Piece Section on cutting mat right side up. Place Two Piece Section right sides together to first. **Wide D strip is across top.** Lock seam.

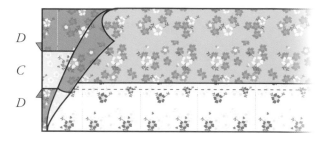

D

C

D

2. Square left end. Cut into 2½" sections.

Number of 2½" Sections	
Wallhanging	22
Lap	44
Twin	74
Full/Queen	100
King	132

Layer cut 2½" sections.

3. Assembly-line sew pairs together.

5. Assembly-line sew together.

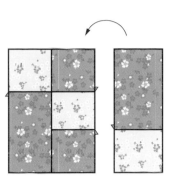

4. Place remaining Two Piece Sections on cutting mat. Layer cut into 2½" sections.

Number of 2½" Sections	
Wallhanging	22
Lap	44
Twin	74
Full/Queen	100
King	132

Cut 2½" sections.

6. From wrong side, press seams in same direction.

Press seams in one direction.

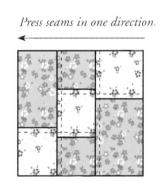

Sewing Blocks Together

1. Count out blocks and set aside for Borders.

Number of Blocks to Set Aside		
	Block One	**Block Two**
Wallhanging	14	14
Lap	20	20
Twin	26	26
Full/Queen	30	30
King	34	34

2. Make two stacks of Block One and two stacks of Block Two. Place equal numbers in each stack. Turn blocks with seams as illustrated so seams lock together.

Number of Blocks in Each Stack	
Wallhanging	4
Lap	12
Twin	24
Full/Queen	35
King	49

3. Flip blocks on right to blocks on left. Lock seams and assembly-line sew. Clip apart between blocks.

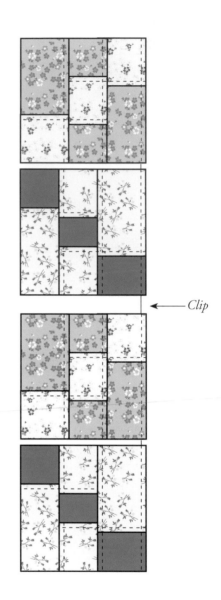

← *Clip*

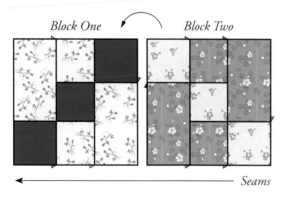

Block One   *Block Two*

← *Seams*

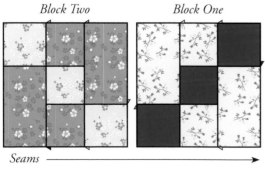

Block Two   *Block One*

Seams →

4. Open. Flip patches right sides together.

5. Push top seam upward and underneath seam downward. Wiggle-match or pin center seams.

8. Open center seam and push down flat to form a tiny Four-Patch.

9. Press new seams clockwise around block.

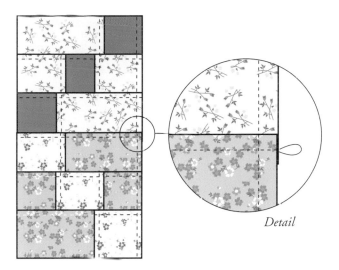

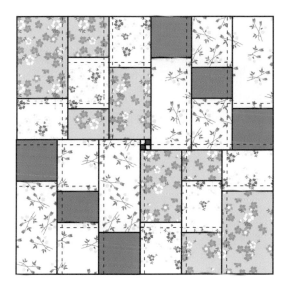

Detail

6. At center seam, cut first stitch with scissors.

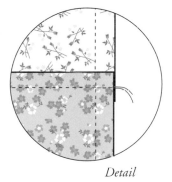

Detail

7. Remove the three vertical stitches at center on both sides with stiletto or seam ripper.

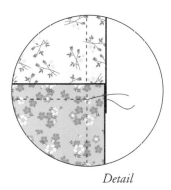

Detail

Sewing Top Together

1. Lay out blocks.

2. Assembly-line sew vertical rows together.

3. Sew horizontal rows. Push seams between blocks in opposite directions.

4. Press from the wrong side, then on the right side.

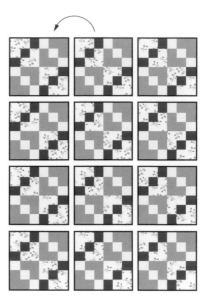

An example of a Lap size quilt

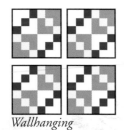

Wallhanging

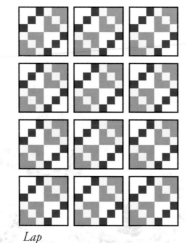

Lap

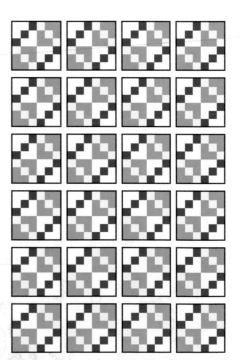

Twin

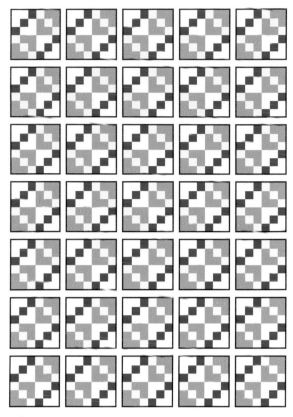

Queen

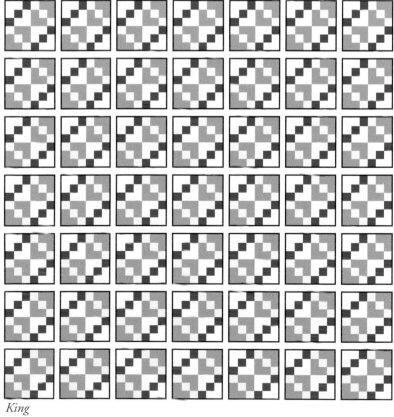

King

Adding Inside Borders

1. Measure several blocks to find average size, approximately 6½".

2. If block measures less than 6½", trim 6½" Inside Border strips to block measurement.

3. Trim selvage edges, and sew together into one long piece.

4. Measure, pin and sew 6½" strips to sides. Set seams and press toward Inside Borders.

5. Measure, pin and sew strips to top and bottom. Set seams and press toward Inside Borders.

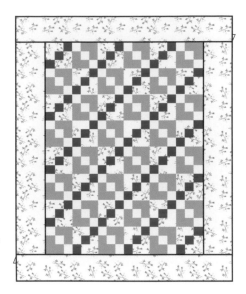

Sewing Two Side Borders

1. Make one stack of Block One and one stack of Block Two.
Turn blocks with seams as illustrated so seams lock together.

Number of Blocks in Each Stack		
	Block One	**Block Two**
Wallhanging	6	6
Lap	10	10
Twin	14	14
Full/Queen	16	16
King	16	16

2. Flip blocks on right to blocks on left. Lock seams, and assembly-line sew. Clip apart between pairs.

Clip apart between pairs.

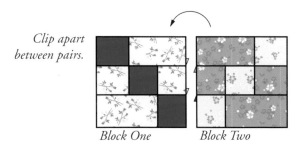

Block One   *Block Two*

Turn blocks with seams as illustrated so seams lock together.

3. Assembly-line sew pairs into two rows of equal blocks.

4. From wrong side, press to the right.

Number of Blocks in Each Side	
Wallhanging	6
Lap	10
Twin	14
Full/Queen	16
King	16

Example of a Lap

5. Pin and sew to sides, repressing indicated single seams.

6. Press seams toward Inside Border.

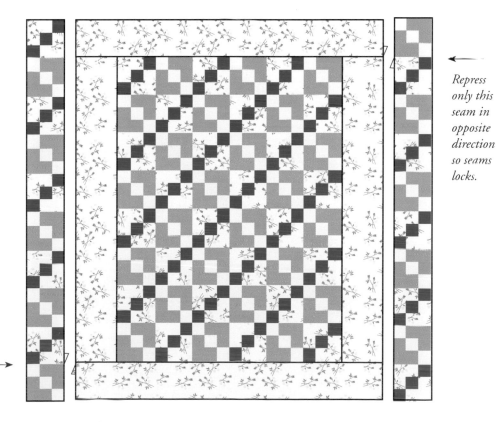

Repress only this seam in opposite direction so seams lock.

Repress only this seam in opposite direction so seams locks.

Sewing Top and Bottom Borders

1. Make one stack of Block One and one stack of Block Two.

Number of Blocks in Each Stack		
	Block One	**Block Two**
Wallhanging	8	8
Lap	10	10
Twin	12	12
Full/Queen	14	14
King	18	18

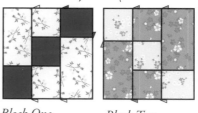

2. **Turn blocks with seams as illustrated so seams lock together.**

3. Flip blocks on right to blocks on left. Lock seams, and assembly-line sew. Clip apart between pairs.

Block One   *Block Two*

Turn blocks with seams as illustrated so seams lock together.

4. Assembly-line sew pairs into two rows of equal blocks.

Number of Blocks in Top and Bottom Rows	
Wallhanging	8
Lap	10
Twin	12
Full/Queen	14
King	18

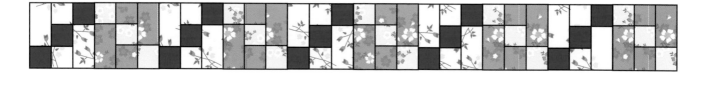

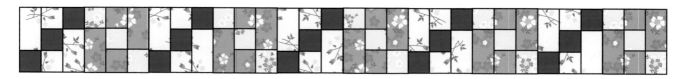

Example of a Lap

5. From wrong side, press seams to the right.

6. Pin and sew top and bottom, repressing indicated single seams.

Repress only this seam in opposite direction so seams lock.

Repress only this seam in opposite direction so seams lock.

7. Press seams toward Inside Border.

8. Turn to **Finishing Instructions** on 226.

Don't Fence Me In Quilt

I am so fortunate to have a little "ranch" in rural Julian, California, up on Volcan Mountain. It's only nine acres, but for California, it's a ranch! When my workweek is done, I head for Julian and fresh air!

Give me those wide open spaces that I love, beside my best friend Brian with fishing poles in our hands. Let me be by myself in the evening breeze, picking ripe juicy blackberries, and turning them into sweet jam. Let me listen to the murmur of the blowing oak trees, hiking with two grandpuppies, and swimming in the pond. Baking bread, picking wild flowers, planting apple trees, quilting on the porch - don't fence me in.

Eleanor and Brian pose "American Gothic" style in front of Eleanor's log home in Julian, California. In contrast to the irony and realism of Grant Wood's 1930 original painting, Eleanor can't conceal her joy of living in the country and delighting in the freedom it offers.

Fabric Selection

Marie was not "fenced in" on her lap size quilt! She used rich, warm jewel tones and echoed them with black and white to create her vibrant zig-zag effect.

Pieced and Quilted by Marie Harper 56" x 78"

Eleanor outfitted the "ranch" with this warm flannel quilt, made in traditional John Deere prints. She's ready to snuggle by the fire when those cold winds blow.

Pieced and Quilted by Eleanor Burns 56" x 79"

Pieced by Eleanor Burns
Quilted by Pat Wetzel

56" x 78"

First
Dark

354-30

First
Dark Medium

356-05

First
Light Medium

First
Border

350-30

Same
Light

355-30

Second
Dark

Second
Border

350-84

Second
Dark Medium

352-84

Second
Light Medium

354-84

Same
Light

355-30

Third
Border

350-48

How to Select Your Fabric

Select two different color families. For each family, select the first fabric as Dark, and the next two fabrics progressively lighter for Dark Medium, and Light Medium. Select the lightest fabric, Same Light, to use with both color families. In the finished top, the two Darks and the Same Light stand out.

In the example quilt, gold lightens light gold with blue flowers, and buttercup. The Same Light features petite roses with buttercup and blue blossoms.

In the second color family, progression begins with deep teal, into teal with gold flowers, and light teal.

Yardage

Finished Block Size 8" square	Wallhanging 4 x 4 =16 total 40" x 40"	Lap 5 x 8 = 40 total 56" x 78"
First Color Family Dark *Paste Your Fabric Here*	8 Blocks ¼ yd (2) 2½" strips	20 Blocks ⅜ yd (4) 2½" strips
Dark Medium *Paste Your Fabric Here*	¼ yd (2) 2½" strips	⅜ yd (4) 2½" strips
Light Medium *Paste Your Fabric Here*	¼ yd (2) 2½" strips	⅜ yd (4) 2½" strips
Same Light *Paste Your Fabric Here*	⅓ yd (4) 2½" strips	⅔ yd (8) 2½" strips
Second Color Family Dark *Paste Your Fabric Here*	8 Blocks ¼ yd (2) 2½" strips	20 Blocks ⅜ yd (4) 2½" strips
Dark Medium *Paste Your Fabric Here*	¼ yd (2) 2½" strips	⅜ yd (4) 2½" strips
Light Medium *Paste Your Fabric Here*	¼ yd (2) 2½" strips	⅜ yd (4) 2½" strips
First Border *Paste Your Fabric Here*	⅓ yd (4) 2" strips	½ yd (6) 2½" strips
Second Border *Paste Your Fabric Here*	½ yd (4) 3½" strips	⅓ yd (6) 1¾" strips
Third Border *Paste Your Fabric Here*		1¼ yds (7) 6" strips
Binding *Paste Your Fabric Here*	½ yd (4) 3" strips	¾ yd (7) 3" strips
Backing *Paste Your Fabric Here*	1½ yds	4¾ yds
Batting	46" x 46"	62" x 86"

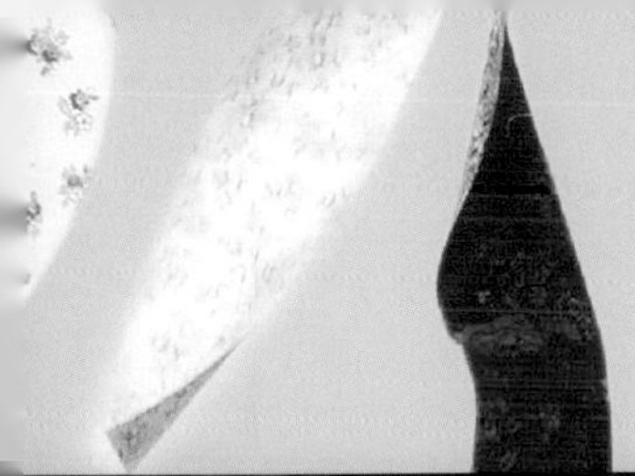

Twin	Full/Queen	King
6 x 10 = 60 total 70" x 98"	9 x 10 = 90 total 90" x 98"	10 x 12 = 120 total 98" x 114"

30 Blocks
½ yd
   (6) 2½" strips
	45 Blocks
	¾ yd
	   (9) 2½" strips
		60 Blocks
		1 yd
		   (12) 2½" strips

½ yd
   (6) 2½" strips
	¾ yd
	   (9) 2½" strips
		1 yd
		   (12) 2½" strips

½ yd
   (6) 2½" strips
	¾ yd
	   (9) 2½" strips
		1 yd
		   (12) 2½" strips

1 yd
   (12) 2½" strips
	1½ yds
	   (18) 2½" strips
		1¾ yds
		   (24) 2½" strips

30 Blocks
½ yd
   (6) 2½" strips
	45 Blocks
	¾ yd
	   (9) 2½" strips
		60 Blocks
		1 yd
		   (12) 2½" strips

½ yd
   (6) 2½" strips
	¾ yd
	   (9) 2½" strips
		1 yd
		   (12) 2½" strips

½ yd
   (6) 2½" strips
	¾ yd
	   (9) 2½" strips
		1 yd
		   (12) 2½" strips

¾ yd
   (7) 3½" strips
	1 yd
	   (8) 3½" strips
		1⅛ yds
		   (10) 3½" strips

½ yd
   (8) 1¾ strips
	½ yd
	   (9) 1¾" strips
		¾ yd
		   (10) 1¾" strips

2 yds
   (9) 7½" strips
	2¼ yds
	   (10) 7½" strips
		2½ yds
		   (11) 7½" strips

⅞ yd
   (9) 3" strips
	1 yd
	   (10) 3" strips
		1⅛ yds
		   (11) 3" strips

6 yds	8½ yds	9 yds
74" x 106"	100" x 106"	108" x 124"

Sewing Blocks

1. Line up 2½" strips from First Color Family.

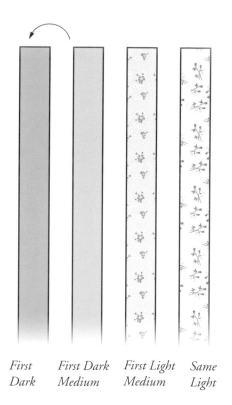

First Dark

First Dark Medium

First Light Medium

Same Light

Press first seam toward Dark Medium.

Press second seam toward Light Medium.

2. Assembly-line sew strips together.

3. Press after each strip is added.

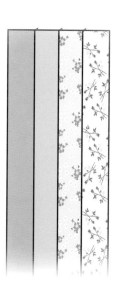

Press final seam toward Same Light.

4. From wrong side, check that all seams are pressed toward Same Light.

5. Place on cutting mat. Square off left edge.

6. Measure width of strips.

7. Cut strips that measurement into squares. You should get five squares from each set of strips.

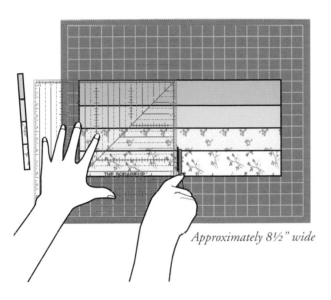

Approximately 8½" wide

9. Repeat strip sewing for Second Color Family.

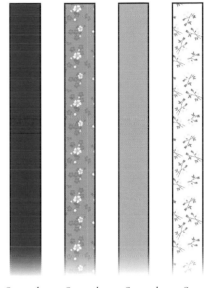

| *Second Dark* | *Second Dark Medium* | *Second Light Medium* | *Same Light* |

8. Cut this many squares.

First Color Family	
Wallhanging	8
Lap	20
Twin	30
Full/Queen	45
King	60

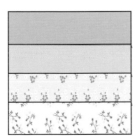

Approximately 8½" square

10. Cut strips into squares.

11. Cut this many squares.

Second Color Family	
Wallhanging	8
Lap	20
Twin	30
Full/Queen	45
King	60

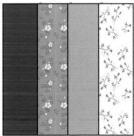

Approximately 8½" square

Laying Out Top

1. Lay out blocks.

2. Sew vertical rows together.

3. Sew remaining rows, locking seams.

4. Add borders.

5. Turn to **Finishing Instructions** on page 226.

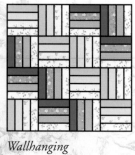

Wallhanging

Lap

Twin

"Nothing runs like a Deere," and there is nothing more fun than running up a quick 2½" strip quilt on a sewing machine!

Full/Queen

King

One Pillow Sham

Double yardage if you intend to make two shams. Sham can be made with or without scallop.

27" x 33"

Finished Size 27" x 33"		
Paste Your Fabric Here	Main Fabric	1¾ yds (1) 28" x 34" top (2) 21" x 28" backing
	Batting	1 yd (1) 28" x 34

Making Sham

1. Hem one 28" side on both backing pieces.

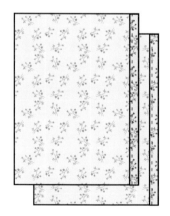

2. Place backing pieces right sides together to top piece, overlapping hems in center. Match outside edges.

3. Place on top of batting, with backing wrong side up. Pin.

4. For straight edge, sew ¼" seam around outside edge.

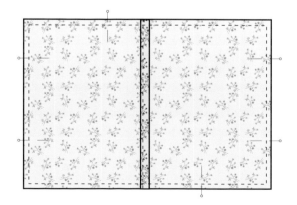

Scallop Edge Only

1. Trace scallop template on page 83 onto template plastic and cut out.

2. Draw 45° lines on four corners of backing piece.

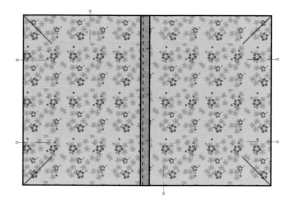

3. Place corner of scallop template on diagonal line. Trace inside of scallop with marking pen.

4. Move and mark scallops from two ends toward middle. Make adjustment in center scallops to fit. You may need to elongate or shorten scallop.

5. Sew on scallop line. Trim ¼" away from stitched line, and clip curves.

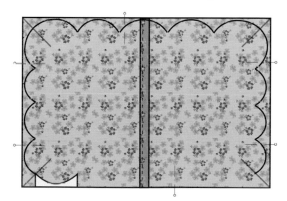

Finishing Sham

1. Turn right side out.

2. Mark stitching line 3" from straight outside edge, or 3" from top of scallop.

3. Quilt on line.

4. Stuff with pillow.

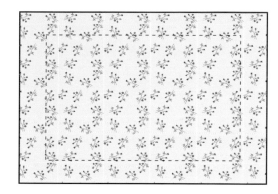

Finishing Your Quilt

Sewing Vertical Rows Together

1. Lay out blocks in order.

2. Flip second vertical row right sides together to first vertical row.

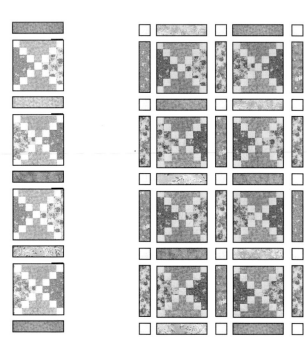

3. Stack from bottom up with top block on top of stack.

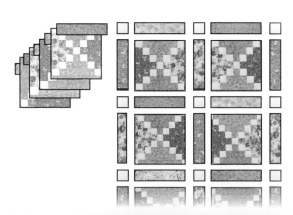

4. Assembly-line sew. Stretch or ease each block to fit as you sew. Do not clip connecting threads.

5. Open vertical rows one and two.

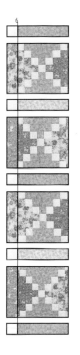

6. Stack third vertical row. Flip pieces in third row right sides together to pieces in second row while assembly-line sewing. Do not clip connecting threads.

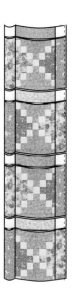

7. Repeat with all vertical rows.

8. Lay out quilt. Check that every block is in its proper position.

Sewing Horizontal Rows Together

1. Flip top horizontal row right sides together to second horizontal row. Stretch blocks to meet, and sew.

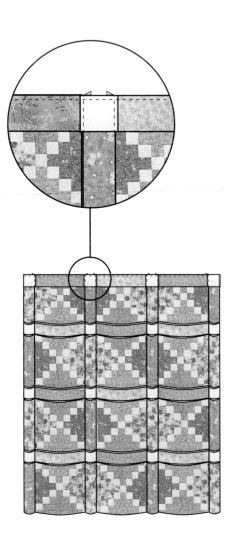

2. Where pieces are joined by threads, match seams carefully. Push seams for locking seams.

3. Continue sewing all horizontal rows.

4. Press from wrong side. Press on right side.

Adding Borders

1. Cut Border strips according to Yardage Charts.

2. Trim away selvages at a right angle.

3. Lay first strip right side up. Lay second strip right sides to it. Backstitch, stitch, and backstitch again.

4. Continue assembly-line sewing all short ends together into long pieces.

5. Cut Border pieces the average length of both sides.

6. Pin and sew to sides. Fold out and press seams toward Border.

7. Measure the width and cut Border pieces for top and bottom. Pin and sew.

8. Press scams toward Border.

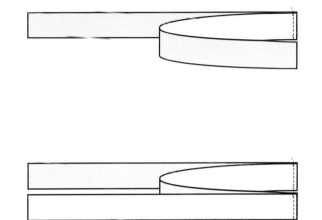

Layering the Quilt

1. If necessary, piece Backing.

2. Spread out Backing on a large table or floor area, right side down. Clamp fabric to edge of table with quilt clips, or tape Backing to the floor. Do not stretch Backing.

3. Layer the Batting on the Backing and pat flat.

4. With quilt right side up, center on the Backing. Smooth until all layers are flat. Clamp or tape outside edges.

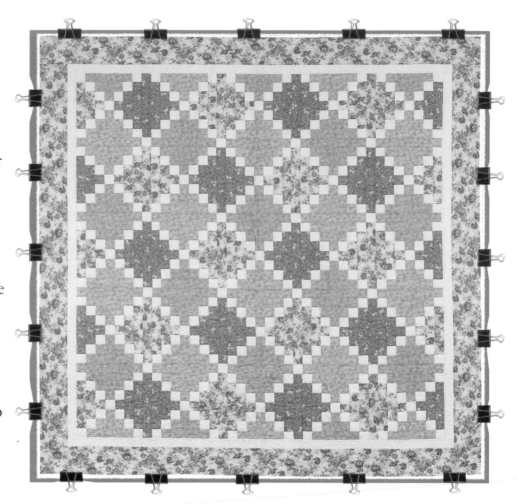

Safety Pinning

1. Place pin covers on 1" safety pins. Safety pin through all layers three to five inches apart. Pin away from where you plan to quilt.

2. Catch tip of pin in grooves on pinning tool, and close pins.

3. Use pinning tool to open pins when removing them. Store pins opened.

"Stitch in the Ditch" along Blocks and Borders

1. Thread your machine with matching thread or invisible thread. If you use invisible thread, loosen your top tension. Match the bobbin thread to the Backing.

2. Attach your walking foot, and lengthen the stitch to 8 to 10 stitches per inch or 3.0 on computerized machines.

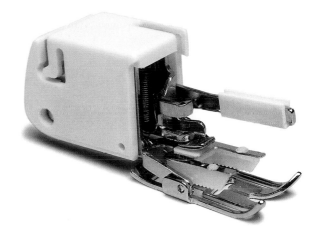

3. Tightly roll quilt from one long side to center. Place hands on quilt in triangular shape, and spread seams open. Stitch in the ditch along seam lines and anchor blocks and border.

4. Roll quilt in opposite direction, and stitch in ditch along seam lines.

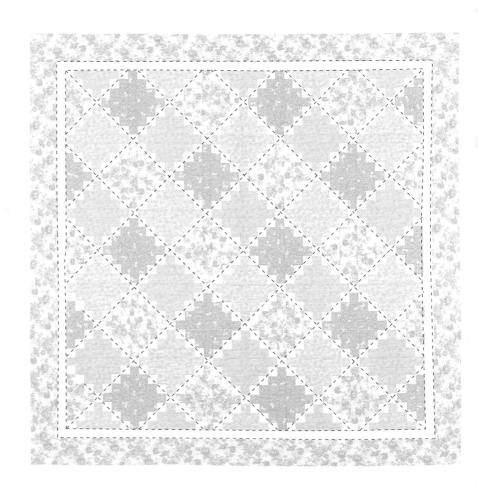

Quilting Blocks with Darning Foot

The advantage to using a darning foot to quilt is that you don't need to constantly pivot and turn a large heavy quilt as you do with a walking foot.

1. Attach darning foot to sewing machine. Drop feed dogs or cover feed dogs with a plate. No stitch length is required as you control the length. Use a fine needle and invisible or regular thread in the top and regular thread to match the Backing in the bobbin. Loosen top tension if using invisible thread. Use needle down position.

2. Plan how to stitch, covering as many seams continuously as possible.

3. Place hands flat on block. Bring bobbin thread up on seam line.

4. Lock stitch and clip thread tails. Free motion stitch in the ditch around block. Keep top of block at top. Sew sideways and back and forth without turning quilt.

5. Lock stitch and cut threads. Continue with remaining blocks.

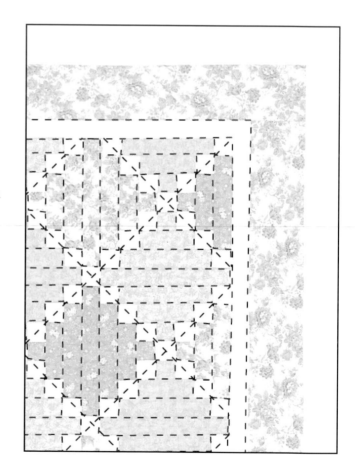

Marking for Free Motion Quilting

1. Select an appropriate stencil.

2. Center on area to be quilted, and trace lines with disappearing marker. An alternative method is lightly spraying fabric with water, and dusting talc powder into lines of stencil.

3. Attach darning foot to sewing machine. Drop feed dogs or cover feed dogs with a plate. No stitch length is required as you control the length. Use a fine needle and invisible or regular thread in the top and regular thread to match the Backing in the bobbin. Loosen top tension if using invisible thread.

4. Place hands flat on sides of marking. Bring bobbin thread up on line. Lock stitch and clip thread tails. Free motion stitch around design. Lock stitches and cut threads.

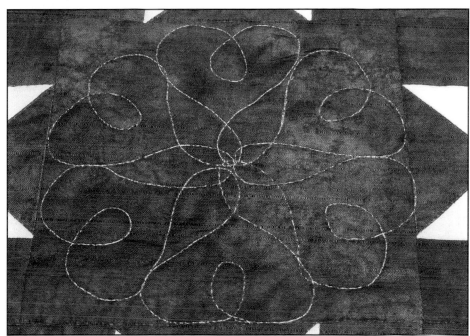

Binding

Use a walking foot attachment and regular thread on top and in the bobbin to match the Binding.

1. Square off selvage edges, and sew 3" Binding strips together lengthwise.

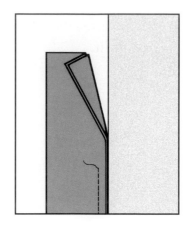

2. Fold and press in half with wrong sides together.

3. Line up raw edges of folded Binding with raw edges of quilt in middle of one side.

4. Begin stitching 4" from end of Binding. Sew with 10 stitches per inch, or 3.0 to 3.5. Sew ⅜" from edge, or width of walking foot.

5. At corner, stop stitching ⅜" in from edge with needle in the fabric. Raise presser foot and turn quilt to next side. Put foot back down.

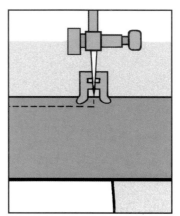

6. Stitch backwards at an angle off the edge of Binding.

7. Raise the foot, and pull quilt forward slightly.

8. Fold Binding strip straight up on diagonal. Fingerpress diagonal fold.

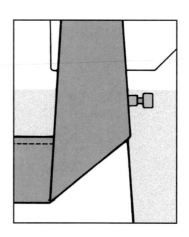

9. Fold Binding strip straight down with diagonal fold underneath. Line up top of fold with raw edge of Binding underneath.

10. Begin sewing from edge.

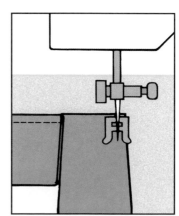

11. Continue stitching and mitering corners around outside of quilt.

12. Stop stitching 4" from where ends will overlap.

13. Line up two ends of Binding. Trim excess with a ½" overlap.

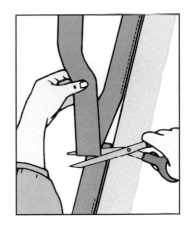

14. Open out folded ends and pin right sides together. Sew ¼" seam.

15. Continue to stitch Binding in place.

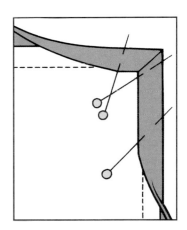

16. Trim Batting and Backing up to raw edges of Binding.

17. Fold Binding to back side of quilt. Pin in place so that folded edge on Binding overlaps stitching line. Tuck in the excess fabric at each miter on the diagonal.

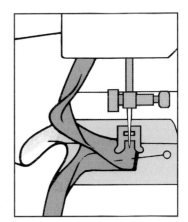

18. From right side, "stitch in the ditch" using invisible thread on the front side, and a bobbin thread to match the Binding on back side. Catch folded edge of Binding on back side with stitching. Optional: Hand stitch Binding in place.

19. Sew an identification label on Back. Embroidered labels make a nice touch.

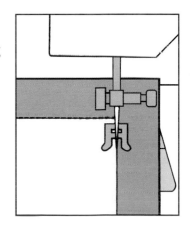

Acknowledgments

Thanks again to family, staff and teachers who helped make my quilting dreams a reality. I will always treasure the memories of our happy times together. I couldn't have had twenty-five wonderful years without you!

A grateful thank you to all these quiltermakers for their participation in Still Stripping.

Sue Bouchard
Judy Callahan
Linda Fornaca
Robin Green
Marie Harper
Debra Jenks
Patricia Knoechel
Nancy Letchworth
Nancy Loftis
Julia Markovitz
Laurie McCauley

Linda McKenna
Linda Parker
Amie Potter
Carol Selepec
Loretta Smith
Peggy Stinson
Sandy Thompson
Amber Varnes
Teresa Varnes
Neta Virgin
Gloria Yankin

All Students who took my Twenty-fifth Anniversary Test Classes

Life is just a bowl of Cherries!

Pieced by Eleanor Burns
Quilted by Teresa Varnes
45" x 45"

Index

Order Information

Quilt in a Day books offer a wide range of techniques and are directed toward a variety of skill levels. If you do not have a quilt shop in your area, you may write or call for a complete catalog and current price list of all books and patterns published by Quilt in a Day®, Inc.

Easy

Bits & Pieces Quilt
Courthouse Steps Quilt
Double Pinwheel
Easy Strip Tulip
Flying Geese Quilt
Flying Geese Quilt in a Day
Irish Chain in a Day
Make a Quilt in a Day Log Cabin
Nana's Garden Quilt
Northern Star
Rail Fence Quilt
Star for all Seasons Placemats
Trip Around the World Quilt
Winning Hand Quilt

Snowball Quilt
Star Log Cabin Quilt
Trio of Treasured Quilts
Triple Irish Chain Quilts
Wild Goose Chase Quilt

Applique

Applique in a Day
Dresden Plate Quilt
Sunbonnet Sue Visits Quilt in a Day
Spools & Tools Wallhanging
Dutch Windmills Quilt
Grandmother's Garden Quilt
Ice Cream Cone Quilt

Holiday

Christmas Quilts and Crafts
Country Christmas
Country Flag
Last Minute Gifts
Log Cabin Wreath Wallhanging
Log Cabin Christmas Tree Wallhanging
Lover's Knot Placemats
Patchwork Santa
Stockings & Small Quilts

Sampler

Block Party Series 3, Quilters Almanac
Block Party Series 4, Christmas Traditions
Block Party Series 5, Pioneer Sampler
Block Party Series 6, Applique in a Day
Block Party Series 7, Stars Across America
Star Spangled Favorites
Still Stripping After 25 Years
Town Square Sampler
Underground Railroad

Intermediate

Bears in the Woods
Birds in the Air Quilt
Boston Common
Delectable Mountains Quilt
Fans & Flutterbys
Friendship Quilt
Intermediate
Jewel Box
Kaleidoscope Quilt
Lover's Knot Quilt
Machine Quilting Primer
May Basket Quilt
Morning Star Quilt

Angle Piecing

Blazing Star Tablecloth
Pineapple Quilt
Radiant Star Quilt

Quilt in a Day®, Inc. • 1955 Diamond Street • San Marcos, CA 92069
1 800 777-4852 • Fax: (760) 591-4424 • www.quiltinaday.com

Pieced by Teresa Varnes
Quilted by Carol Selepec
50" x 50"

Pieced by Eleanor Burns
Quilted by Teresa Varnes
21" x 38"

Pieced by Eleanor Burns
Quilted by Teresa Varnes
16" x 16"

Nine-Patch and Stripe

Look closely at these magical quilts! Mirror image blocks are made for these two quilts at the same time! They are perfect for two beds in the same room, or, finished with entirely different setting fabrics, the quilts can be used in two different areas.

Sue Bouchard stitched up these two rich looking quilts for a cozy hideaway corner in El's log home. Long arm quilter Neta Virgin put her talents to the test, and finished them off in grand style.

Quarter Log Cabin

In 1978, Eleanor self-published her first book, the Log Cabin, and was off to a stripping start. Now, 25 years later, she presents a fun variation on the pattern that's just as easy for beginners to make. These Quarter Log Cabin blocks are built from the corner, rather than the center, and each fabric is used only once. Choose lights and darks with a high degree of contrast for a dramatic look. Teresa Varnes started with the Deep Rose fabric from Eleanor's Yours Truly line to build her cozy-looking quilt in reds and greens. Carol Selepec quilted it with feather motifs and background stippling. All backgrounds and greens are from the Yours Truly line.

Pieced by Teresa Varnes
Quilted by Carol Selepec
84" x 84"